To Marty

A fellow practitioner of the "ARTS"

Continued success

[signature]

META-TALK

GUIDE TO

HIDDEN MEANINGS

IN CONVERSATIONS

Gerard I. Nierenberg
and
Henry H. Calero

SIMON AND SCHUSTER · NEW YORK

To Roy, Roger, George, Yolanda and Frances

CONTENTS

FOREWORD

"Do you still love me?"
"Of course, I love you."
"Then why don't you talk to me?"

"What do you think my chances are, Doctor?"
"I'll do my best."

"When I was your age . . ."
"I'm going out."

"Are you getting anything out of this?"
"I'm living with you. What more do you want?"

"I earn my money. Why can't they?"

Isn't it possible to hear behind and beyond the literal meanings of these much-used expressions? In daily life our conversation says both much more and much less than is intended. For these meanings behind our ordinary talk we have coined the word "meta-talk." Our study of meta-talk is not an exercise in how to gain an advantage from the hidden messages we can hear in talk. Our principal goal is to promote better relations between people. To do this it is necessary to understand how meta-talk blurs and confuses our communication process.

Although the word meta-talk is new, the methods of discovering and analyzing it are not. We have followed the pioneers in the fields of philosophy, psychology, semantics and general semantics, linguistics, and communication. Also, we have utilized the observations of thousands of our seminar participants who have given us their understanding of the meta-talk they have encountered in their day-to-day conversations.

To simplify this book we have identified the words, phrases, and usages that make up meta-talk and have described some of their deeper meanings. Each usage is then collected under the various relationships and situations in which it most commonly occurs. This does not mean that these types of meta-talk are found only in the limited areas to which we refer. Indeed, meta-talk in all its variations is to be found in every relationship and life situation we encounter. As a caveat, always consider that no meaning is ever absolute. Meaning is in the speaker, listener, and circumstance.

i

ANOTHER LANGUAGE: META-TALK

Oscar Wilde, a known conversation plagiarist, on hearing James McNeill Whistler making a witty remark: "I wish I had said that."
Whistler: "You will, Oscar, you will."

Why do so many of us fail to communicate effectively? Why do people continually ask, "What did he say?" when they are neither hard of hearing nor below average intelligence? The reasons may be as diverse as the people involved in the process, but a few stand out: effective talk is a blend of many skills evolved over a long learning period. It cannot be forced into early bloom anymore than a child can be made to speak before he is ready. Listening is another stumbling block. Although we must listen before we can talk, many of us forget this elementary fact and listen, if at all, only to the sound of our own voice. Others adopt certain words and phrases and repeat them over and over like a child who has learned a new word or an adolescent with the latest bit of teenage jargon. Correspondingly, many fail to listen for meta-talk, the meaning behind the words they hear. This can be as limiting as being able only to say and comprehend "*oui*" while in France.

A mother mouse and a baby mouse were out walking one day. Suddenly, a cat jumped out to corner them. The mother mouse said "Bow wow," and the cat ran away. The mother turned to the baby and said, "See the advantage of knowing an extra language?" Understanding meta-talk is like knowing an extra language.

The Levels of Talk

"Then you should say what you mean," the March Hare went on.

"I do," Alice hastily replied; "at least—at least I mean what I say—that's the same thing, you know."

"Not the same thing a bit!" said the Hatter. "Why, you might as well say that 'I see what I eat' is the same as 'I eat what I see'!"

—Lewis Carroll

In the office of a California lawyer is a sign: "I know you believe you understand what you think I said. But I am not sure you realize that what you heard is not what I meant."

The statements underline some of the problems involved in talk. Talk would present relatively few problems if it involved only the apparent meanings of the words that we use. However, this is not the case. Talk exists on at least three levels of meaning: (1) what the speaker is saying; (2) what the speaker thinks he is saying; and (3) what the listener thinks the speaker is saying. The first level requires little consideration; here we are simply dealing with the words a person uses, without considering how they are understood. The words do not in themselves carry any emotional messages. They are like the transcript of a court-room trial, stripped of all emotional context. The way a person says "How do you do?" can convey many different messages, but written down, the words themselves do not reveal "what" has been said. The circumstances and context would have to be known before we could give depth of understanding to the multiple possibilities.

The second and third levels require much more consider-ation than the first. Here is where the differences may arise; while the speaker thinks he is being understood on one level, the listener may be listening on an entirely different level. Illustrating the confusion that can arise is the story of the grandmother who tells her teen-aged granddaughter, "There are two words I don't want you to use. One is 'swell' and the other is 'lousy.'" "Okay, Grandma," says the girl, "what are the two words?"

In earlier days, when the formal study of communications was just beginning, many people said, "What we need is better communication." They felt that this alone would break down the barriers between people. In some instances they were probably right. In others, however, the listener may understand the speaker only too well and that, too, can cause difficulties. The speaker may say something that on the surface appears quite innocuous, when, as a matter of fact, that is the impression he wants to give in order to divert the listener from the importance of the words. How-ever, the listener may understand the speaker's intentions and understand him at a deeper level. Lovers, husbands and wives learn this early in their relationships. This greater understanding actually improves communication, but it does not necessarily resolve difficulties. It may cause more. We should not, however, stop at this point. We agree that greater understanding in communications is advantageous and add that it also can lead to new difficulties. However, it is nonetheless true that a still further increase in our understanding may eventually eliminate some of these new difficulties.

There are still other problems involved in understanding talk. It is possible that a message is not necessarily complete on any or all of the three levels. Although it is not our intention to determine what may be true in a particular situation, we will consider the types of mental gymnastics that a speaker and a listener may go through to determine meaning. It is easy to appreciate their difficulties. As an example, a basic precept of general semantics is that "the word is not the thing." This means the object can never be the same as the word that designates it. The word is merely a symbol. We should not expect the same nutritional value from the menu as from the food it represents. On another level the same holds true of phrases that we use. They abstractly symbolize feelings, attitudes, emotions and the like. Even the same person using the same phrase twice may intend vastly different meanings. Think of the many differences that exist between a speaker and listener—cultural coloring, personal connotations, the predigested emotions and intellect which are poured into every phrase used. They almost justify our frequent inability to transmit clear meanings.

WORN-OUT TALK THAT BETRAYS:
CLICHÉS, PLATITUDES, AND TRUISMS

"What we are destroying is nothing but houses of cards
and we are clearing up the ground of language on which
they stand."
                                        —LUDWIG WITTGENSTEIN

Stale, worn-out phrases and expressions, known as
clichés, are frequently used by people too lazy or unimagi-
native to perceive a situation and describe it freshly. Clichés
can be thought of as verbal tics. They are convenient because long use has made them acceptable. However, these
pre-packed sentiments never quite fit the immediate situation. They lack the type of mental challenge which furthers
communication. A cliché usually elicits a reaction of mere
silence or the mouthing of another cliché.

One instructive account of how clichés distort communication was that given by Senator Thomas Eagleton after the
1972 Democratic presidential nominations. He explained
that his only contact with Frank Mankiewicz, a top aide of
George McGovern, about the Vice-Presidential nomination
"was the thirty-five seconds I spent on the phone with him
after Senator McGovern called me to be his running mate.
Mankiewicz said, 'No skeletons rattling around in the
closet, right?' and I said, 'Right.' "

Eagleton interpreted the skeleton-in-the-closet cliché as
it is usually understood, meaning concealed gross mis-
conduct. Therefore he answered Mankiewicz' second cliché,
"Right?" with the cliché that is required: "Right!" Mankiewicz probably did not expect "Wrong" and did not get it.
Mankiewicz knew at that time that Eagleton had been
hospitalized for mental depression, yet felt "it wasn't a

serious problem." When later informed of this, Eagleton said, "They sure didn't let me know about it." If he had known that they were concerned about this as a political liability, he commented, "I would have said, 'That's right. The reports are true. That's the way it is.'" Thus a breakdown in communication was due to the use, or rather misuse, of a cliché.

A single word when used expressively and for a certain effect can become a cliché. One such is "incidentally," used to introduce a statement. This, and the companion phrase, "by the way," should mean and are intended to mean, "Just by chance I happen to think of this." These are relatively harmless devices often used by people who are shy or unsure of themselves. They want to work up the courage to say what they mean. When you hear them you probably should blame yourself for failing to recognize the previous verbal and nonverbal signals which indicated that the other person had something which he considered important to say. They are also used where the person wants to mislead you into thinking that what he has to say is unimportant.

Take as an example an editor who is having a brief conference with a writer. After a few preliminary remarks the editor says, "Incidentally, that Churchill story will have to come out." A brief pause while the writer asks a silent "why?" Editor: "My boss doesn't like it. He thinks you've made too many assumptions." Writer: "I didn't make them. Churchill did." The editor pauses. "Well, we'll see."

Again, there has been a breakdown in effective communication. Here the "incidentally" indicates the point that the editor is about to make is important to him. Blaming his boss, however, could be an attempt to minimize his own involvement in the judgment (or it could be the simple truth, but it nonetheless creates an uncertainty in the writer's mind). The positions of the two men, although they are standing close to each other, emphasize a certain distance between them. They are not talking face to face. They are addressing their words to the typewritten copy as indicated by a soft, reflective tone of voice on the part of the editor, and there is, of course, no eye contact. Verbally and nonverbally, no effective communication has taken place. This is confirmed by the cliché, "Well, we'll see," which means, "decision postponed." Thus the writer can spend futile hours asking, "What did he mean?" Without further information, he will never know.

Platitudes, aphorisms, maxims, and the like are major candidates for a cliché-ridden conversation. The sentiments expressed can be misleading. Take for example, those favorite observations at wakes, "Here today, gone tomorrow," and "God takes those first He loves best." In the event of a sudden death they are apt if not very comforting, but if used at the funeral of an 89-year-old woman, they sound grotesquely funny.

One trouble with familiar sayings is that they act as a brake to effective communication. They offer instant wisdom that does not lend itself to verification through logic or experience. Very often the sayings contradict each other: Married in haste, we may repent at leisure vs. A stitch in time saves nine; He who hesitates is lost vs. Fools rush in where angels fear to tread; Look before you leap vs. Faint heart never won fair lady. The worldly wisdom that is allegedly yours through the use of stale expressions that have become clichés is neither worldly nor wise. "You can't teach an old dog new tricks" has kept many a person from attempting a new and potentially rewarding change in his life. The only thing he is left with is the realization that he will never know if he was or wasn't equal to the challenge. "Don't rock the boat" has sunk many an enterprise because of excess caution when a creative alternative was available. Even if a person gets by "Don't rock the boat," he will be discouraged and probably stopped by "You can't fight City Hall," or that other cliché, "That's just the way things are."

Examine the words and phrases that you use to excess. They have become clichés for you at least, no matter how aptly they may be used by other people. A good exercise is to rearrange suspected clichés. Would you, for example, be more likely to read a newspaper article headlined "You Can't Fight City Hall" or one topped with the headline "You Can Fight City Hall"?

Many years ago schoolchildren were forced to memorize what they considered a dreadfully dull poem of Longfellow's called "The Arrow and the Song." Someone finally relieved the monotony by juxtaposing the first two lines with a later line, producing these results:

> I shot an arrow into the air,
> It fell to earth, I knew not where.
> Later I found it in the heart of a friend.

A similar device is to change the position of a single element in a sentence. Watch what happens in the following riddle and answer: What is harder than getting a pregnant elephant in the back seat of a car?—Getting an elephant pregnant in the back seat of a car.

Clichés are given new life with a fresh twist, as: "Behind every successful man is a woman with nothing to wear"; "A man's castle is his home if he is president"; or "Noisy barrels are also lighter."

Altering a cliché may make it more bearable to the listener, but better still, if possible, discard them. Approach each new life situation with a fresh viewpoint unshackled by "trite truisms," "stale aphorisms," and "verbal tics."

How to Get Close to Others— Immediacy and Distance

"Speech is the picture of the mind."

—John Ray

An additional reason for finding clichés objectionable is that they put a certain distance between reality and what we say. In *How to Read a Person Like a Book* we explored the gestures that indicate like and dislike. In some cases the degree of like or dislike can literally be measured by the actual distance between the speaker and the listener. Albert Mehrabian in *Silent Messages* has made use of what he calls "the immediacy principle" to evaluate how people react to others. He says, "People are drawn toward persons and things they like, evaluate highly and prefer; and they avoid or move away from things they dislike, evaluate negatively, or do not prefer." Physical movement (or lack of it) of the eyes and the body can reveal how one person responds to another. A speaker would prefer the eyes of his audience to be focused on him rather than glancing aimlessly about the room. He would prefer that the audience crowd around him after his speech rather than rush for the nearest exit.

Meta-talk can also indicate likes and dislikes, not by actual statements of preference but by (1) order of words, (2) choice of words, and (3) grammatical usage.

(1) Order of Words

The order in which we refer to things shows our preferences. The things we say first are more important. Try asking someone what he would like to eat for dinner. See his preference. If you know a couple to whom you refer by first names, notice whom you name first. Is that person more important to you than the other? Chances are that it is true.

(2) Choice of Words

The use of personal pronouns, for example, provides a valuable clue. First person pronouns, "I" and "we," are verbally closer than "he," "she," and "it." "They" is the most remote of all, while "we" used collectively is the most immediate. Contrast "*We* do it and we like it!" with "*They* do it and they *like* it." The first sounds like a perhaps unusual but socially acceptable pastime; the second could apply to anything from wife-swapping to cannibalism, but it definitely implies disapproval. Often a person's deepest prejudices are revealed by his use of "they" because it opens up such a great gulf between the speaker and "them." "It's them against us" is often implied in such remarks as, "What do *they* want?" and "I earn my money. Why can't *they*?"

(3) Grammatical Usage

Since verbs express action or state of being, they can mirror with fair accuracy the degree of closeness or distance of feeling between the speaker and the person or object spoken about. To the traditional grammarian, mood, tense and voice indicate quite clearly the immediacy or distance in time or place of an act. For example these various tenses are in descending order of immediacy: present, past, perfect, pluperfect. Or to put it into a situation any child would understand at once: "We are going to the circus"—present—(yes); "We went to the circus"—past (happened once, maybe again); "We have gone to the circus' —perfect—(happened once, probably not again); "We had gone to the circus"—pluperfect (happened once, not again). The future tense often depends on other elements in the sentence to indicate whether it is near or distant future: "We shall go to the circus Monday" (near future) vs. "We'll go to the circus some other time" (never). Voice also indicates distance. "I have made my decision" (active voice) is more immediate than "The decision was made by me" (passive voice). Finally, the mood (mode) of a verb does the same. The subjunctive mood, used in a conditional clause or to express desire, is much more remote than the indicative used to express a fact. The use of the subjunctive, however, has become so rare in the United States that many would be hard put to think of a single example. They would probably know instinctively that "If I were king" is correct and "If I was king" is not, but that is probably as far as it goes. The British still preserve some real and implied usage of the subjunctive. This can be seen in dealings with shopkeepers. They respond readily to "Might I have some?" and adversely to "Give me some." However, this has little relevance for meta-talk. The use of the subjunctive relies on a precise understanding of the English language and is a conscious choice. Curiously, Americans use the past subjunctive in a way that does have a meta-talk meaning. To the Englishman "Would you do this?" (subjunctive) represents a softening of the request, as opposed to "Will you do this?" (indicative). To an American familiar with "polite" bosses, it is just the reverse: "Would you?" is a command; "Will you?" implies a choice.

Modern language students have discarded many of the elements of traditional grammar. Certainly a number of artificial distinctions in traditional grammar have long since vanished from popular usage. "I shall," "you will," "he will," were once used to connote a statement of fact; "I will," "you shall," "he shall," indicated determination. Popular usage has done away with many of the old-fashioned grammatical theories and the English language is somewhat less precise because of it. But the distinctions of immediacy are still fairly obvious and intuitively grasped. We will deal with these distinctions in future chapters. Like clichés they reveal more about what a person is saying than he may realize.

LIFE AS A LISTENING POST

> "If I can listen to what he tells me, if I can understand how it seems to him, if I can sense the emotional flavor which it has for him, then I will be releasing potent forces of change within him."
>
> —CARL ROGERS

No book on talk could be whole without a few observations on listening. Talking and listening are opposite sides of the same coin. For golden words to be of value, the sender and receiver are required to be equally proficient in totally different procedures and skills. Just as in the pressing of a coin, pressure must be applied equally to both sides or an imperfection will result, both parties in a conversation must exert all their efforts whether in listening or talking.

Otherwise communication between them will be flawed. We should not be able to talk without listening, yet there are many who do. A psychologically insecure person may talk continuously to keep people away. He chatters incessantly hoping that no one can penetrate his defenses, a constant barrage of talk. Others refuse to stop talking in a conference for fear that they will lose control of the negotiation. A person anxious to persuade another may never stop to listen long enough to know if he is getting through. Very often he is not. A young teacher learned this with her first class. She was very concerned that the class know what to do during a fire drill. She reported, "I kept repeating the directions at every opportunity. Just before the actual fire drill I spent another half hour on instructions. Then I said, 'Is it clear to everyone?' A little boy spoke up: 'We would be able to understand much better if you didn't try to explain so much.'" Finally, there is the person who is so enamored of his own ideas that he does not conceive that the other party's thoughts might assist him or aid the conversation. These are some of the barriers to listening. It is most important to overcome them.

Listening abilities are of several types and they exist relatively independently of each other. A person may be very skillful at listening for recall, yet he is not necessarily skilled in evaluating or thinking critically about what he has heard. One college professor describes the first type of listening as belonging to the "professional" student. A person who possesses excellent recall may very well get an "A" in a course, but may miss the greater benefits of education: creativity, which can be helped by critical listening and evaluation.

In another form called nondirective listening, the listener attempts to do the following:

1. *Take time to listen.* Whenever he senses the speaker has become emotional and needs to talk things out, he lets him.

2. *Be attentive.* He concentrates on what the speaker is saying and uses gestures such as tilting the head slightly to indicate nonverbally that he is paying attention.

3. *Give the speaker feedback.* Again he uses nonverbal communication to indicate approval—a smile or nod of the head is often all that is necessary.

4. *Not probe for additional information.* There is a distinct difference between willingness to listen and curious intent. Probing often causes the speaker to withhold information he would otherwise reveal.

5. *Not be critical.* He refrains from passing judgment on what is being said.

6. *Refrain or postpone giving advice.* If asked for advice, he holds off, realizing that the speaker may evolve his own solution during the course of the talk.

7. *Respect the speaker and his worth.* He makes the speaker feel important and worthwhile, but at the same time does not diminish his own image.

One must keep silent in order to learn how to speak. Yet, although listening is a primary obligation of talking, this, too, has its problems. People have become extremely sophisticated in matters involving communication. One seminar participant complained that he disliked dealing with another individual because he always "tried the art of listening on me." Whatever techniques we use, we must consider all the possible results and effects upon each specific listener. They also should be chosen for appropriateness to a given situation.

Sometimes a conversation can change in a matter of seconds from simple statements and questions to a highly charged argument. The speaker's words have triggered emotions completely unrelated to the speaker's intent. Such situations are the lifeblood of soap operas. Let's look in on Fred (father-in-law) and Gloria (daughter-in-law) talking about Julie (a friend of both) who has a marital problem.

> FRED: I want you to talk to Julie about her problem with her husband.
> GLORIA: I'm not sure I can help her.
> FRED: Sure you can. She is being very unreasonable with her husband.
> GLORIA: Your son and I also have our disagreements.
> FRED: But they aren't the same as theirs.
> GLORIA: I'm sure they are. You just are not aware of them.
> FRED: Don't tell me I don't know what's going on.
> GLORIA: You *don't* know. How could you? I'm the one who lives with him. You try living with him. I quit!

The problem here is that neither has listened to or been aware of the emotional content of the other's dialogue. Listening has as much to do with sensing emotions as hearing words. After this exchange, retreat would be almost impossible for either Fred or Gloria.

These are some of the symptoms of a poor listener:
1. Early rejection of the subject because:
   A. It is uninteresting.
   B. It is already known.
   C. It is too complicated.
   D. It is too simple.
2. Considering aspects of the speaker other than what he is saying.
3. Permitting the mind to be captured by a segment of the speech, thereafter cutting off continued response.

4. Selective perception. People are prepared to see or hear what they expect.

The following are two examples of selective perception:

A man reading the newspaper says to his wife, "What do you think of this? The navy is going to have women serving aboard ship."

"Wait until the Women's Lib movement hears about that! They're going to be very angry."

"Why should they be angry?"

"Watch what's going to happen. If women have to serve lunches and dinners on board ship, the men are going to get as much flack as they would get at home."

"No, no. That's not what the article said. It means that women would serve their country by sharing duty with the men, not that they would become servants."

The wife had expected to hear something about women's rights and the linking of "women" and "serving" started a totally erroneous train of thought.

At a shoeshine parlor in a northern airport the following scene took place:

A man sat down and, with a deep southern accent, asked for a shine. The black attendant looked at him full face and asked, "What *kind* of shine do you want?" The southerner became very defensive. He answered, "What does *that* mean?"

It appeared that his expectation of what he might expect from a northern black was coming true.

With this the attendant pointed to a huge sign directly in front of the customer which read:

Shines
Regular   35¢
Wax   45¢
Glaze   75¢

The southerner answered shyly, "Regular." Although he had been looking straight at the sign during the entire conversation, he had not read it.

ii

PUTTING THE LISTENER
IN A FRAME OF MIND

A friend of ours was negotiating with a firm that makes bio-feedback machines—machines that measure minute nerve impulses, brain waves, and other biological phenomena. He went to California to attend a business meeting which would determine whether or not he and the company executives could work together. Before the meeting formally began the president very proudly showed our friend a machine they had just begun to produce. It measured the muscular tension of a person's arm. Using our friend as a guinea pig, they attached his right arm to the machine to illustrate how difficult it is to achieve a really relaxed state. After about fifteen minutes, however, he was able to achieve almost total relaxation. It then occurred to him that this would be a good time to discuss his future relationship with the company. The president could observe by looking at the machine dial any increase in tension. They discussed their future relationship and the role that each would play. The readings of complete relaxation indicated by the machine as he talked convinced the firm members of our friend's sincerity, and the deal was consummated.

Few negotiators are fortunate enough to have their opposition machine-read for them. However, awareness of meta-talk can provide strong clues of how the negotiation is going. This chapter will enable you to recognize the phrases used to prepare the mind of the listener.

HIDING THE HALO: ARROGANCE AND FALSE MODESTY

"Fair words make me look to my purse."
—GEORGE HERBERT

People are usually reluctant to say right out: "I am good, I'm very good," although they might agree wholeheartedly with the statement. Some are prevented by modesty, others by fear of derision from their audience. When the group is made up of presumed social equals, such a statement would be met with concealed or even open resentment at the bad taste of the speaker. Even if the speaker is of superior social status or a public figure, the remark annoys those listening.

It is doubtful that anyone today would openly make an arrogant comment like William Henry Vanderbilt's "The public be damned." But the emotion is still there, ready to be expressed in many covert ways. One of the simplest is use of the royal third person singular. If you hear Senator Joe Smith say, "Joe Smith would never take that course. He knows how the people would suffer," you are back in the seventeenth century hearing the monarch say, "It is the king's desire . . ." This mannerism indicates a massive ego, but one that is easily shattered.

The regal "we" is a similar device. It is sometimes hard to separate the regal "we" from the "we" as a group. If you are not included in a "we" there is a good chance that you are being patronized—or worse. If your boss says, "We have decided that you are not strong enough to be department head," he is not trying to soften the blow. He wants to put as much vertical distance between the two of you as he can manage. Transforming the straightforward "I" to a lofty "we," besides distorting human relationships, maims the English language. Compare, for example, John Paul Jones' "I have not yet begun to fight" with Queen Victoria's "We are not interested in the possibilities of defeat." Today if given a choice, most would eagerly follow Jones and leave the queen all alone.

Some arrogant people are less sure of themselves than the would-be kings and queens. They use self-deprecating words to convey a modesty they do not feel. Dickens' character Uriah Heep is a celebrated caricature of this group. "There are people enough to tread upon me in my lowly state," Uriah says, "without my doing outrage to their feelings by possessing learning. Learning ain't for me. A person like myself had better not aspire. If he is to get on in life, he must get on 'umbly." And his mother, Mrs. Heep, choruses: "'Umble we are, 'umble we have been, 'umble we shall ever be."

Despite this devastating example from more than a hundred years ago, there are people today who attempt to conceal their arrogance by denying it.

If someone were to stand before you on a raised platform, stretch his frame to its fullest height, hold onto his coat lapels with both hands, and say, "I'm not boasting, but . . ." chances are that you would not believe him to be humble. If this is so, then why do so many use this type of expression? They still believe that people can be fooled by false humility and their meta-talk reveals their contempt for their audience.

Recently an expert was asked to testify regarding the possibility of anticipating earthquakes along the San Andreas fault in California. He started his testimony with the expression "In my humble opinion . . .," which drove the person asking the question into a rage. He shouted, "We are not interested in your false humility, we are seriously concerned about future earthquakes and determining where and when they may occur. Please tell us what you believe to be the best approach to the problem."

The expert, visibly shaken, squirmed in his seat, adjusted his pants, sat up straight, and replied sternly, "At present, no one can accurately predict where or when an earthquake will occur on the surface of this planet."

Variants on "In my humble opinion" are: "I do the best I can"; "Far be it from me to say"; "After all, I'm only your mother"; "I know I'm a terrible person"; "Don't tell me what I have to do"; "For him, that's pretty clever"; "I'm only a woman"; "If you ask my opinion"; "It's not that I'm . . ."; "I'm not boasting, but . . ."

The meaning of the meta-talk can vary with the situation and the person using it. However, the elements of meta-talk generally add up to a consistent message. A recent advertisement offered a good example of what we mean by consistency. It featured a woman who is a fairly well-known decorator, but mentioned her name only, not her profession. The reader was supposed to know her profession—an example of how silence can be used to indicate status. The lady professed to be very much concerned about air pollution. "In my own way I've done what I could do," she said with due humbleness. What did she do? She stopped using the three fireplaces in her handsome townhouse. It is not difficult to guess that the real message was "I am rich and successful," not "Stop air pollution."

False humility is also present in the use of the expressions "As you are aware" and "As you well know." The phrases seem to suggest that the speaker is not taking any chances of insulting the listener's intelligence by saying something he is already aware of. This is often not the case. For example, a scientist while telling his colleagues about his newest discovery may say, "As you are aware," knowing full well they are not aware. Rather than softening the blow, he draws sharp attention to their ignorance and sets himself apart from them. Often such an attempt at showing superiority does not go unchallenged.

During a recent national labor-management stalemate, a member of management told a newsman, "As you are aware, the union has called off negotiations." The newsman shot back, "No, I didn't know nor does any other newsman covering this strike know." A politician before an investigating committee began his answer to a sharply worded question with, "As you probably know . . ." The individual asking the question promptly crossed his arms in a defensive gesture, listened to the complete answer, then, pointing his index finger, shouted angrily, "You know damn well I don't know anything about that."

The expression is occasionally used not as a cliché but as a statement of fact. For example, a business executive in a meeting with his staff may begin, "As you well know," and follow with specific information, perhaps that their share of the market is slowly slipping away to a competitor. The expression is used legitimately here and serves to focus attention on a subject that one wants to stress.

SOFTENERS, FOREBODERS, CONTINUERS, INTERESTERS, AND DOWNERS

Mickey Deans, Judy Garland's last husband, sent her daughter Liza a copy of his book about her mother with a note saying, "I hope you like it." Before reading the book, Liza recalled, she felt like sending back a note saying, "What if I don't?"

Softeners

Most of us at some time have prefaced our words with expressions intended to influence the listener in a positive manner. We call them "softeners." In such situations we might say, "You're going to like what I'm about to tell you" (preparing the listeners for what we believe will be good news for them); "It goes without saying . . ." (attempting to get agreement before stating something); "What I'm about to tell you . . ." (usually a disclosure that must be handled very carefully and usually involves the listener); "I venture to say," "Don't take me seriously," or "I'm sticking my neck out." Sometimes "off the top of my head" or "at first blush" is used instead and means the same thing.

"Would you be kind enough to . . ." is a softener expression that attempts to influence another with praise or flattery. "I'm sure someone as intelligent as you . . ." strokes a person's ego, as does "You're very perceptive about . . ." "What is your expert opinion of my . . ." asks for concurrence, not censure, as the individual who tells that speaker he disagrees will soon learn. No one uses such expressions looking for negative responses. The meta-talk is: "I've scratched your back and you should scratch mine."

"You are right but . . ." attempts to avoid conflict by feigned agreement. Acceptance statements often are followed by the incongruous qualifiers—"but," "yet," "however," and "still." They communicate that the person does not feel you are right, but would like to soften the blow. A husband arguing with his wife about his conduct at a social gathering says, "You are right, I shouldn't have done that, but . . ." then he explains the logic and reason behind his behavior. Instead of contrition, justification is the theme. This in turn is supposed to make his wife defensive, but usually her gestures signal that she is turned off and sticking with her original judgment. A young professional baseball player who does not take to coaching tells his manager, "You are right. I shouldn't have thrown a curve ball but . . ." then starts demonstrating how it was that he decided to throw a breaking pitch rather than the high, hard one, as the manager shrugs his shoulders, thrusts his hands in his back pockets, and calmly listens while nodding his head in token agreement. Seldom do we encounter someone who says, "You are right," and lets it go at that. Even less often do we find a person who follows "You are right" with "What should I have done?"

Foreboders

Often we put listeners in a negative, anxious frame of mind with the use of "foreboders." As an example when we say, "Nothing is wrong," we mean "There is something wrong. However, I don't want to talk about it."

Similar foreboders that have a negative effect on the listener are: "It really doesn't matter" (it sure does); "Don't worry about me" (please do); and a statement Oliver Hardy used to make to Stan Laurel, "I have nothing more to say," before lashing out at him verbally and physically.

Continuers

Expressions that attempt to get the listener to disclose his thoughts might be called "continuers." High on this list is "What else is new?"—an attempt to get others to talk. This question is often used in negotiating situations, particularly by winner-take-all negotiators. They also tend to use expressions such as: "Go on"; "Now you're talking"; "That's very good"; "I like that." All act as incentives to keep the other person talking. But is this necessarily good? It depends on the motive behind the encouraging remarks. Talk for the sake of talk has probably never damaged a relationship, but continuers used for entrapment are positively malignant. When the trap is sprung it is sometimes accompanied by a triumphant, "You said it. I didn't." (And that may be followed by the protest, "That's not what I meant at all!") The player of this game makes all the rules and "wins" when he gets the other person to say what he wants him to say. The victim, however, seldom feels bound by these arbitrarily imposed rules and nothing is accomplished. Better a shared conversation than one dominated by an egotist or an unwilling dupe.

Interesters

The following statements and questions attempt to arouse the interest of the listener.

"And do you know what he said?" This is a strong plea for interest and is used to get undivided attention. Used once or twice it is very effective, but eventually it no longer creates interest but rather boredom or even distaste. We begin to anticipate the question, no longer listening but waiting for its repetition. It becomes a game and we may count the number of times the question is asked in order to keep our sanity. This phrase often becomes a verbal tic, revealing the speaker's feeling of insecurity. There is an alternate use of this phrase. It is sometimes used to get con-currence from another, particularly in a conflict situation where the speaker wants a third party's approval: "After all I've done for him, do you know what he said?" The person supplies information about his feelings and attitude, usually complimenting himself and hoping to influence the other to support his position.

"Guess what happened?" When this question is used the listener is subtly being told to ask, "What?" so that in complicity with the speaker he will share an unimportant bit of information. The question really does not give the listener a choice—it demands his attention. As such, it is frequently resented and may elicit a facetious answer that stops the conversation dead in its tracks with the questioner angry and the answerer feeling guilty. Basically the question reveals that the speaker is uncertain that he has anything relevant or interesting to say.

"Did you hear the one about . . . ?" This question in-structs the listener to conceal any knowledge of the joke that will follow. He also is instructed to become interested and get ready to laugh. A "yes" is not expected; the question is merely an attempt to put the listener on the alert. The trouble with this phrase is that it more often than not is followed by a boring story and that is what the listener expects when he hears the question. If he meekly says, "No," he is bored; if "Yes," he offends. In effective communication a story flows naturally from the conversation and does not need this limping question to introduce it.

"What do you think of . . . ?" This query calls for interest and agreement. A political cartoon recently showed two women in conversation with one asking, "What do you think of the soak-the-rich tax program?" The reply was, "A mild dose of 'soak the rich' and 'share the wealth' is in the noblest of our political traditions." The questioner frowned, rejecting the response. The reason is that the question is often used to insist on agreement with the speaker's opinions. For the meta-talk expert, then, "What do you think of . . . ?" is followed by insights into the foibles and prejudices of the person who uses it.

"I could say something about that." This statement can cause both interest and conflict. In a discussion between two persons, a long-suffering soul who resists disclosing his true feelings may utter this expression only after a long sigh to demonstrate his patience. Yet the person who dislikes conflict attempts not to fuel arguments by using such trite phrases, remaining silent instead. On the other hand, the I-don't-want-to-cause-trouble-but-will-anyway type tends to use this expression. He draws attention to a conflicting statement or issue by seeming to avoid a confrontation. "I could say something about that" may provoke the response, "Well, why don't you?" Then the fight is on.

When two individuals are discussing a third person's plight, one may use the statement to create interest not conflict. It then signals the beginning of a gossip session. The statement usually gets an immediate reaction from the listener because he realizes that some disclosure is about to be made. The politician who uses it, however, commits a serious *faux pas*, because voters want him to reveal his feelings and state his position openly. Although he may use many expressions to sidetrack, sidestep or generally not answer questions, this statement is one an astute politician seldom uses.

Downers

Persons involved in win-lose situations describe winning over someone in statements heavy with meta-talk worthy of a caveman hunter: "That got him"; "That did him in"; "That took him down a peg"; or "That beat him into the ground." And when they want to tell you something they believe you are very sensitive about, they say, "I know you don't like to discuss it. . . ." Then when you get angry, they say, "I was only trying to help."

The following downers are used intentionally to put the listener in a defensive state of mind.

"How about . . ." In numerous negotiating situations individuals using this phrase arouse extreme tension in an otherwise cooperative environment. Most of us have the emotional stability to handle one, two, or even three "How abouts." However, when the phrase is repeated again and again, the cumulative effect serves to make us defensive, angry, and sometimes irrational. "How about" is a buzz phrase for many of us and serves to stimulate our opposition to the person uttering it.

"Are you happy now?" This question is the cry of a poor loser. It is intended to put the listener on the defensive for having caused the speaker so much humiliation and anguish. The implication is that he is a sadistic brute. In a typical American marriage, the question is asked by one partner after the other has delivered a blow to his or her ego. "Are you happy now that you've ruined my evening with your antics?" the wife may ask, after the husband has flirted with most of the women at a party. Or a husband may use the same question to protest his wife's conduct after divulging the family's precarious financial position, his insecure job status, and, in general, the economic gloom hanging over their heads.

"Don't make me laugh." Laughter is not only a message of good-humored acceptance. It also can be a rejection. The expression "Don't make me laugh" is a mean-hearted reaction to another human being's request or demand. It effectively cuts off all further communication and should be avoided.

"Don't be ridiculous!" heads the list of commands beginning with "Don't." The person saying it is authoritarian, incapable of seeing any colors except black and white. Very few listeners would resent a command that makes sense ("Don't walk on the grass"; "Don't smoke in bed.") But, "Don't be ridiculous!"? Is one supposed to abjectly renounce all his characteristic ways to please the person making the demand? Not likely. "Don't be ridiculous!" usually prompts the question, "What do you mean ridiculous?" This continues the downward spiral of the conversation that will probably end in angry words or blows.

"Needless to say . . ." Sandor Feldman believes that this statement reveals "ambivalence of feelings, envy or jealousy covered by positive love feelings." This is the case when one person admonishes another for his actions and then states, "Needless to say, your ethnic or religious background has nothing to do with our opinion." Similar to this is, "I have many (black, white, brown, etc.,) friends." If it is unnecessary to say something about the other person's background, why say it? Could it be that we feel that it is

necessary to state a socially acceptable position even when
we disagree with it?

The phrase can also convey a sense of superiority or a
self-righteous dedication to one's own beliefs. The wife who
angrily reacts to her husband's forgetting their wedding
anniversary might berate him by saying, "Needless to say,
I married a man with an extraordinary memory for special
occasions." Responding to her meta-talk, he quickly asks,
"What day is it?" or "What's the occasion?"

The marketing manager addressing his sales force during
a period when their company's percentage of the market is
dwindling might say, "Needless to say, we have the most
aggressive sales team going. That is why we are slowly becoming number two in the industry."

"Needless to say, we would all like to be handsome and
rich." Or would we? Sometimes we project our own feelings
and needs on others by using this phrase. Because we feel
very strongly about something we want others to share our
feelings and we take the liberty of assuming they do. If you
say, "Needless to say, everyone needs goals in life," you can
watch many of the younger generation squirm. However,
"Needless to say, everyone should do his own thing" brings
but approving smiles.

ATTEMPTS AT LOGICAL REASONING [CONVINCERS]

"To give a reason for anything is to breed a doubt of it."
—WILLIAM HAZLITT

A Kentucky judge, after hearing a moonshining
case, said to the defendant, "Although you were not caught
using it, we found equipment on your premises capable of

producing alcohol. We are therefore going to find you guilty." To that the defendant replied, "Now that you mention it, you might as well also convict me of rape. I've got all the equipment for that too."

Reasoning logically, our remote ancestors came to the conclusion that the world was flat. Today we still use verbal logic to justify our proof and strengthen our attitudes, preconceived ideas, notions, and assumptions. "Doesn't everyone?" is commonly asked when a person's conduct or morals are called into question. A young boy was once persuaded by his friends to go on a stealing escapade. Since he liked excitement, he joined them. They were discovered, chased, and one was caught—the young lad. When he was asked why he was stealing in spite of the fact that he obviously had ample money, he replied, "All the other kids are doing it." Adults use the same justification when they say, "It was *only* politics" or "That's the *only* way we can do business in this city."

One of the most irritating comments that can be made is "Why, anyone can do it!" when you have been asked to do something and voice doubt about your ability. It implies that the task is so simple even a moron could successfully tackle it. "Anyone can follow my line of reasoning" attempts to persuade by intimidation, although it is cloaked in the logic of "I find it simple, therefore it is simple, therefore anyone can grasp it." Another similar device appeals for consensus by threatening ostracism from the group: "I think we all agree that . . ." These phrases and statements may unconsciously express contempt for the listener, but one thing that is perfectly clear is that "Let me make one thing perfectly clear" has introduced many a conscious deception that openly shows contempt for the listener's intelligence. Others abandon any pretense at logical persuasion with strong-arm expressions such as "I'm not suggesting anything" (no, they're *telling* us) or "Don't be unreasonable" (a judgment from on high).

Meta-talk in advertising which is intended to prove logically the superiority of a product or service bears close scrutiny. As an example, a well-known manufacturer of a cold remedy was asked by the Federal Trade Commission to substantiate its advertising claim that "summer colds are a different type of animal." The company's response was that they had had a survey made and found that that was what people thought. Listen for the hidden messages in advertising commercials. They often say far more than the ad men intend.

Understanding and Using
Needs and Values [Strokers]

"Reason is nothing but the analysis of belief."
—Franz Schubert

Many who have used a strong-arm approach have assumed that their opposition's needs are the same as their own. As a result, in attempting to influence others, they themselves have been influenced against their wishes. Take the case of Lord Brandon and his wife, which also involved William Lamb, later Lord Melbourne, Prime Minister and advisor to Queen Victoria. Brandon came across an exchange of letters between his wife and Lamb that indicated their friendship had developed into a much more ardent relationship. Brandon wrote his wife and told her of his discovery, adding that he was quite willing to forgive a momentary indiscretion if she would use her influence with her bedmate to get him a bishopric. His wife replied that she would degrade neither herself nor her *friend* by making such an appeal, but that she was very glad to retain in her possession a letter in which such a suggestion was made. Moral: When attempting to influence, be aware of the other person's needs and sense of values. They are not necessarily the same as yours.

Frustration is revealed in such statements as "What's the use." That is shorthand for "I can't cope with this anymore." In this case, the inflection of the voice rather than the words themselves indicate the state of mind. A rising pitch would signal a question: "What's the use?" A person with ready answers would be likely to ask such a question. He will take the positive approach that solutions to the problem are available. A falling pitch, on the other hand, states that nothing can be done about the situation. Similarly, "Forget it" can be the equivalent of "You're welcome" or "Don't mention it" if said in a friendly way. But if the tone of voice is bitter, it means, "You haven't listened to what I said, so I refuse to talk any more about it." "You win" indicates that the speaker and the listener both have the idea that communication is a game where one wins and the other loses. Effective communication cannot take place at this level, so this statement is not only a sign of frustration, it should be regarded as a signal to stop playing games and try to accomplish something.

Self-doubt is revealed in the many expressions that plead with the listener to accept without question the veracity of everything that the speaker has to say. "Believe me," "I'm not kidding," "I *have* to tell you," "I wouldn't lie to you" have little value except as communication stoppers. Probably everything that follows is going to be a lie or a half-truth. Recently, two men on a flight to Los Angeles were in a heated argument over their company's loss of valuable information to a competitor. One man spoke in a low tone but the other roared his opinion that "X" had stolen the secret information. The loud-voiced man said, "Believe me, I have such evidence you wouldn't believe it." But when pressed, he could only cite hearsay and ill-founded rumors. All statements, however, were prefaced with "Believe me." Finally his companion, sensing that the conversation was being overheard, terminated it by saying coldly, "Okay, I believe you. Let's drop the subject." The constant "Believe me's" had merely reinforced the other man's disbelief and increased the speaker's self-doubt.

Hostility in communication often indicates weakness. "Mind your own business," "Stay out of this," "The matter is closed," "I don't want to hear any more" and other abrupt attempts to terminate a conversation can frequently be traced to the fact that the speaker feels he has lost an argument. He tries to regain control of the situation by displaying his power to choose what will or will not be discussed. In one of Hank Ketcham's *Dennis the Menace* cartoons, Dennis' mother says, "The subject is closed," and her son explains to a playmate, "That means I won the argument, but I don't get nothing."

One company president was able to accomplish the same results nonverbally. When a subordinate pressed an argument too forcefully, the president would turn off his hearing aid and sit smiling at the baffled subordinate. This worked perfectly until he ran into a stubborn employee who also wore a hearing aid. When the boss turned off his hearing aid the employee did the same and a grinning match developed. The impasse was broken by a curious secretary who wondered about the unusual silence. She looked into the office, realized at a glance what was happening, brought in coffee and left without saying a word.

Reassurance is often the desired result of such questions as "How do you like my new outfit?" "What do you think of my plan?" and "I didn't go too far, did I?" The last thing the speaker wants is criticism, yet we often give a double-barreled reply that tries to reassure yet criticize at the same time: "I like it very much but . . ." This communicates that the person is critical, not that he is reassuring. In this situation it is better to be critical or reassuring rather than give a compliment, then take it away. That reinforces the blow. In the interest of effective communication, it is probably better to understand the meta-talk and answer the true question that was asked, and criticism is not the answer. Many times upon getting the reassurance that he needs, a person will become his own best critic. Two women were discussing new styles in women's clothes. One said, "By the way, what do you think of my new outfit?" The other could have truthfully replied, "It's very nice but you're too fat to wear it." Instead she answered the question that had been asked: "It's certainly in style." The one who needed reassurance then remarked, "I know I'm overweight, but I just couldn't resist buying it." No doubt these two women will remain friends for a long time.

Denial of good fortune is often a device used by superstitious people to avert the evil eye. It is also used by some to pretend that things are better than they actually are. An example of the second type is the man who asks, "You don't think something's happened, do you?" when he means, "I think something's happened!" A third type of denial seeks information while pretending to be above mere curiosity. If a person says, "Please, I don't want to hear any gossip or idle rumors," he probably means, "Just give me the sordid facts." Still others deny they have an overwhelming desire to give information. Every neighborhood has one member who makes it his or her business to know what's going on. He weighs every bit of information seen, heard, read, or intuitively felt and is ready to tell all, introducing it with: "God forbid that this should get around . . ." "You won't believe it but . . ." "I shouldn't tell you this . . ." "Don't breathe a word of this . . ." And finally there are those who deny they are saying what they truly mean to say. "It's not the money, it's the principle of the thing" is meta-talk for "It's the money."

DEALING WITH EMOTIONS [PLEADERS]

Envy is often mirrored in meta-talk of the "sour-grapes" variety. "*I would never do that*" can mean "I'd do it if I had the opportunity." Two middle-aged women sat in a hotel lobby watching a well-shaped young woman in a tight-fitting blouse and obviously not wearing a brassiere walk by them. One said, "Isn't that disgraceful!" Her companion smiled and maintained a discreet silence, realizing that the real message was, "I wish I had what she has." Silence is probably the best policy in such cases, although, if it can honestly be given, reassurance is even better.

Envy is such a universal emotion that it is easy to be cynical about any statement beginning, "I wouldn't want a . . ." Tone of voice and congruent gestures will tell you whether a person is envious of the material possessions of others or whether he gives them a lesser priority in his life.

Self-interest is of course a necessary human characteristic. Everyone must have it at least to some degree in order to survive. It is only when self-interest becomes selfish interest that harm may be done. At the most extreme, "Dog eat dog" and "You asked for it" indicate a person who has virtually cut himself off from his fellow men. Milder cases of self-interest are detected by the degree of emotion invested in the words. For example, during the Eisenhower administration a new term was introduced to indicate an economic downturn: recession. As someone explained, "It's a recession if your neighbor is out of work and a depression if you are out of work."

There appears to be an inconsistency in today's youth counterculture. Much is said about sharing, brotherhood, love, and so forth, yet most often are heard expressions such as "Doing my own thing" and "I did it my way." This same self-interest was evidenced many years ago when a musical artist is supposed to have said "We've talked about me long enough. Let's talk about you now. What did you think of my Carnegie Hall recital?"

Uncertainty about our ability to do a job well may produce meta-talk that indicates we cannot do it at all. An individual who has been asked to undertake a difficult assignment may reply, "I'll do my best" or "I'll try." The boss may wonder about such statements. Does "I'll do my best" mean "My best is none too good," "I can't do it," "I'm not sure I can do it," or what? The same is true of "I'll try." Either statement can prompt the anxious question: "Don't you think that you can do it?" That is because the statements are rationalizations that prepare for failure. The lower the aspirations of an individual, the more probable it will be that he will anticipate failure. Those who are more highly motivated "try" less and "do" more.

Uncertainty about how well he will perform or about what you are thinking may cause a person who thinks he is clumsy to say, "Watch me trip on those stairs." A fat man may say, "Watch me break the chair" as he sits down. These are remarks that are carried over from childhood when by anticipating a disaster one was relieved of embarrassment if it did happen, or one might prevent a thing from happening by magic—if one says it will, it won't. If the statement seems unlikely, your possible response to these remarks is reassurance, as though to a child. If likely, then sit back quietly and witness a real-life disaster happen before your very eyes.

Others prepare for failure by using "if-then" statements: "If you will grant X, Y, and Z, then I'll be able to . . ." This can be a perfectly legitimate statement if X, Y, and Z are realistic requests. Often they are not. They merely serve to interrupt communication and try to place blame for the failure on the other person. The meta-talk here is, "Play the game my way or I won't play well and it will be your fault."

Concealed aggression is a common element in many adult conversations. Polite prefaces are often used to soften pene-trating questions or abrupt statements: "Do you mind if I ask you . . ." or "Have you ever considered doing . . ." These and similar phrases if used sparingly can grease the wheels of communication, but if overused they tend to build up resentment by pressing a point of view too hard. "May I ask a question?" provokes a sullen "No!" when an aggres-sive person signals his desire to dominate the conversation. Patient trust and understanding rather than an ultimatum, however softened, is an effective way to reach agreement.

Although aggressive in their pursuit of criminals, Los Angeles policemen are among the most courteous law en-forcement officers in the country. When they stop a person for whatever reason, they carefully structure their conversa-tion to avoid creating more anxiety than already exists. They make no attempt to build up their own egos by displaying a sense of power or superiority.

An acquaintance of ours in Los Angeles was very proud of not having received a single traffic summons in twenty years, in spite of having been stopped many times. He credited this to his practice of always getting out of his car and meeting the officer halfway. One day, however, he was signaled to pull over on a busy L.A. freeway. He stopped his car, started to get out, and was stopped by a bellow from the officer: "Get back in that car, you fool!" He obeyed. "Sorry for yelling at you," the officer said. "Freeways are not designed for pedestrians. It's very dangerous to walk even for a short distance." Our friend commented, "How could I not cooperate with someone who was really interested in saving my life? Why, I couldn't even bring myself to talk my way out of a ticket!"

Superiority in status, brains, or money is difficult to conceal even if one wants to do so. It may arouse envy in another person. One can usually overcome these differences if he gives proper respect to the attitudes and feelings of the other party. Communication breaks down, however, when the superior person's meta-talk signals condescension. An executive of a large corporation that bore his family's name was explaining a new employee's stock purchase plan. "Of course there is preferred voting stock as well," he said, "but that is family stock and is something that does not concern the employees here." Any good will that the company might have expected from its generous plan was sacrificed as a result of the meta-message: "Preferred voting stock is fine for people like me with a lot of money, but not for you."

Many clichés reveal this abrasive sense of superiority: "That's nothing. You should see . . . ," "As you may remember," "Don't you know that?" and "It may interest you to know . . ." These are but a few of the phrases that say, "I'm richer," "I'm better," "I'm smarter."

Anger and annoyance call into play a whole complex of verbal and nonverbal communication. The voice becomes staccato, gestures more pronounced and negative, and the meta-talk leaves no doubt of the emotion that is felt: "You surprise me!" "What do you mean by *that?*" "Really, this time you've gone too far!" "I could answer that if I wanted to!" "You're impossible!"

No conversation should be allowed to reach this point of no return. The aware person "reads" the words and the gestures that signal a gradual build-up to an explosion. He helps defuse the issue at the first sign of discomfort from his opposer and ensures that the communication is not disrupted. He never has to ask later, "What happened?"

iii

WE LISTEN DIFFERENTLY
SINCE FREUD

"The contribution of psychoanalysis to science consists
precisely in having extended research to regions of the
mind."

—SIGMUND FREUD

Since Freud has become an integral part of our
knowledge, not only has understanding of ourselves and
others changed, but our listening habits have been influenced. We tend to listen with more purpose and attempt
to label more of the things that we listen for. A few of these
labels are: rationalization, projection, displacement, introjection, repression, and reaction formation. Some people
have said that talk is a four-letter word for psychotherapy,
inasmuch as our judgments of other people's actions come
almost solely from their talk. Let us now look at a few examples from everyday life of these psychological labels.

Rationalization

"Men use thought only to justify their wrongdoings.
and speech only to conceal their thoughts."
—VOLTAIRE

Among the recent "sick" stories is one about two
mice sitting in the nose cone of a rocket headed for outer
space. One says, "What a terrible way to die!" The second
says, "Never mind. It's a better way than cancer research."
A similar effort to justify by reasoning after the event can
be found in such statements as "There is no use trying to
reason" or "They would never understand."

A youngster of seven or eight, pursing his lips and saying,
"I don't care about that old thing," is no different from the
executive with high ego needs standing in an authority position, body erect and hands clasped behind his back, loudly
telling his employees, "I don't care that our competitor
received the contract." Both are rationalizing. They attempt
to hide uncomfortable emotions behind a mask of indiffer-
ence. Those who say, "I don't care what people think of
me," often use the statement as a launching pad for a
defense of their conduct elaborate enough to be used at a
murder trial. When "I don't care" is made more emphatic
by adverbs such as "sincerely," "really," or "honestly," the
speaker's true emotions are even more starkly exposed. A
classic case is the jilted lover who says, "Good riddance.
I really don't care about her leaving," while tears well in his
eyes. Everyone can see the emotions that the words try to
hide. Why not say, "I do care about her now and I'm hurt
and humiliated that she treated me this way." Those words

can bring much-needed sympathy, while "I don't care" brings only disbelief.

Sigmund Freud wrote, "The subject matter of a repressed image or thought can make its way into consciousness on condition that it is denied." The word "only" is often used for the purpose of denial. When a person has a nightmare about a subject he does not want to allow to enter his conscious mind, he says, "It was only a dream." The slick ad man insinuates the word into the reader's or listener's mind when he wants to convince that the price in reality is very low: "Only $11.95." The mother who has left her children alone when some tragedy occurred might say, "I was only gone a few minutes." This puts the blame elsewhere, and relieves her of the burden of guilt. Another use is in that often-heard accusation, "If you turn your back on him for only one minute, he gets into trouble." It may be true, but it is not much of an excuse or even a comfort.

Two very religious Jews went to the rabbi to confess they had not kept the fast on Yom Kippur, the Day of Atonement. The rabbi told them they would have to be punished. Then he asked, "Mr. A, what do you like the most?" A responded that he liked sharing his marital bed with his wife. So the rabbi said, "You have to sleep in another bedroom. Stay away from your wife for six weeks. Now, Mr. B, what do you like the most?" Mr. B replied that his greatest satisfaction was smoking his pipe. The rabbi said, "Then you must give up your pipe for six weeks."

Both men understood the punishment and explained it to their wives. Mr. A slept in a separate room and Mr. B put away his pipe. On the third night A's wife knocked on her husband's door. He woke up and understood immediately why his wife was knocking. "But, dear," he said in a despairing voice, "it's *only* the third day. We still can't share our marital bed." The wife replied, "I *only* wanted to tell you Mr. B is already smoking his pipe." (Notice the different degrees of denial in these two uses of "only.")

Projection

We project when we unconsciously attribute to others our own anxious feelings. When we project our feelings of guilt or inferiority on others, we are then justified in our own eyes. Now it is "their" fault. Most people are better able to cope with external enemies than with the nagging of conscience or the tugging of socially unacceptable emotions. "Business is business" is an attempt to show that a person's distorted concept of business ethics are the ethics of the entire commercial community. The projection can backfire on the liar who says, "Everyone lies." He is punished because he can believe no one.

Sometimes in projection the subject can be changed for the object. If someone suddenly accuses you unjustly, saying perhaps, "You hate me!" examine the possibility that he may be saying, "I hate you," and if this seems plausible, it may be wise to go further and find out why. Sometimes projection of our sexual impulses can extend to a group, a race, or a nation. Syphilis, for example, was often called the French disease—except in France, where it was referred to as the Italian disease. It might even be that the Frenchman's reputation as a lover is merely the projection of other, more inhibited, nationalities.

Substituting an acceptable motive for one's baser motive is another form of projection. It would be the height of cynicism on our part to say that everyone who gives generously "out of the goodness of his heart" is merely showing off or has to relieve a guilty conscience, but it could be true of some.

Look closely for projection in all generalizations you encounter in your own and in others' conversation. They often reveal more than one would ever admit. A person's anxiety can be found in a simple statement such as "We are such a happy couple." But be aware that there are at least three ways of reading the comment: "It's true"; "I am happy and I feel guilty about it"; or "I'm afraid my marriage is on the rocks."

Displacement

One winter day a few years ago, a well-dressed middle-aged man was observed trying to extricate his car from a huge snow bank left in the wake of a snowplow. For almost an hour, the rear tires whined as they spun against the packed snow, but the car would not budge. Finally, livid with rage, the man got out of the car and tried to kick the rear fender. Unfortunately, his other foot slipped on the ice and down he went on his back. Completely maddened by the fall, he reached for the nearest object— a brick—and threw it through the car's rear window.

This is an example of one kind of displacement—the relieving of psychological tensions by "taking it out" on an inanimate object. Displacement, however, should not be thought of as only negative. When a socially disapproved act is replaced by a socially acceptable one, the result is displacement, but it is also called sublimation. One would not expect to see a lawyer sucking on a pacifier, but the attorney might receive almost as much oral gratification in successfully arguing a case. The former offers merely sensual gratification while the latter serves a social purpose. Sublimation may be used as a measuring stick for maturity.

There are countless verbal clues as to how well a person has used displacement to master infantile anxieties and become mature. William Steig in *The Lonely Ones* has a cartoon entitled, "Mother loved me, but she died" which is an immature end of the spectrum. At the adult end might be, "It's really not you that I'm angry with." Unfortunately, this comment is seldom heard because we usually do not realize that our anger and frustration are being taken out on an innocent person or object, not the actual cause of our problem. The more often encountered "I hate you" might mean "I hate the boss" or even "I hate myself."

Watch for the verbal clues that tell you how well or how badly others have used displacement in their efforts to grow up. The overly possessive mother, the son who doesn't want to leave home, the Don Juan, the vain woman, all reveal themselves in their talk. You, as observer, can recognize these immature actions and can predict with some accuracy how they will respond to still other life situations.

Introjection

When a young lawyer gets his first case he feels privileged to be offered the opportunity of serving his client. Gradually he identifies with the client so much that whatever happens to the client seems to happen to him also: "They can't do that to us!" He and the client, in the lawyer's mind at least, have become a sort of corporate entity. Objectivity can be lost and emotions dominate the relationship.

Introjection, unconsciously incorporating ideas and attitudes into one's personality, can often be observed in conversation and offers interesting clues to the speaker's personality. "My wife" can be neutral, indicate a close relationship, or suggest extreme possessiveness. Compare it with "the old lady," which denies an emotional involvement and may indicate hostility. "My" school, "my" trade union, "my" home town unconsciously reveal a close attachment to an institution. When we criticize people and institutions, "my" seldom appears in our conversation. Compare "My country right or wrong" with "This country is going to the dogs."

Ideas and attitudes unconsciously incorporated can provide important insights if we are able to trace them to their source. They can tell us what kind of a person a man is (or what he would like to be) by his adopted patterns.

Repression

Depending upon our life experiences, there are various situations and emotions that represent danger to us and that would create anxiety if we should recognize them. So they are subconsciously ignored or repressed. Our eyes do not see them and the other sense organs pass them by. Threatening memories and emotions are similarly repressed. "I forgot" is an excuse used by adults and children. Often the statement is true, but it is no accident that the thing forgotten might not be a happy occasion but one which would cause distress. People who are "accident prone," or who lose things constantly, often have a repressed desire to punish themselves. A mild-mannered person who is repressing hostility may not be uttering an idle threat when he says, "Some day you may push me too far." Many a bully has discovered that repressions can vanish when the threat to ego of a real-life experience is greater than a childhood dread of aggression. The more the emotion has been repressed, the greater the explosion. "Letting off steam" expresses the situation very well.

"Don't get me wrong" is one of the many clues to emotions being repressed. What follows is a neat summary of what the person really desires. Similarly, "I wouldn't want that" is often a verbal denial which means, "I want that very much!" "The last thing I would want to have happen is . . ." gives a great immediacy that would probably surprise even the speaker.

Reaction Formation

The slogan "Support Mental Health or I'll kill you" is funny because it juxtaposes incongruous emotions. Yet reaction formation often takes place when people want to hide an emotion that causes anxiety with exactly the opposite emotion—love for hate, submission for aggression, and so forth. No matter how a person may try to convince you with his extreme politeness, the underlying feeling of concealed disdain may dominate his emotions. Shakespeare excelled in presenting reaction formations. The dialogue prepared by Hamlet for the player-queen, who professes her love for her husband while plotting to kill him, is a vivid example. How can one tell true sentiment from a reaction formation? Hamlet's mother said it all when she observed of the player-queen, "The lady doth protest too much, methinks." The clichés used in polite society and uttered in an artificially enthusiastic manner, are often of this type: "Such a lovely party"; "I just adored your husband"; I couldn't agree with you more." These are invitations to be aware and be prepared for the worst.

PSYCHOLOGICAL PIONEERS

Harry Stack Sullivan

Of the many psychiatrists who have worked in the field of meta-talk, Harry Stack Sullivan and Sandor Feldman stand out. Based upon Sullivan's book *Conceptions of Modern Psychiatry*, and other works, the following is a dialogue that could take place between a doctor and a patient. Between the elements of the dialogue are noted the structure of the question and how it attempts to prevent misunderstanding as a result of an awareness of meta-talk. The situation involves a patient's first visit to this psychiatrist.

DOCTOR: Who advised you to see me?
PATIENT: Doctor A.
DOCTOR: Why did Doctor A advise you to see me?
PATIENT: Doctor A said I was schizophrenic and that you could cure me.

[These questions help to bring out the expectations of the patient. The doctor now has the limits of reality in which he must work: the patient's concept of schizophrenia and what he means by being "cured." It is now necessary to go further in context with reality, and discover why the patient first went to see Doctor A.]

DOCTOR: What brought you to see Doctor A?
PATIENT: My father took me. He thought I should go.
DOCTOR: Why did he think so?

[These questions are attempts to get at the reality of the situation.]

PATIENT: He said I was acting strangely.
DOCTOR: What made him state that you were acting strangely?
PATIENT: I didn't want to go out of the house.

[The doctor is trying to zero in on the basic problems and on the period of time involved. He wants to continue the thought rather than question it.]

DOCTOR: When did you decide that you didn't want to leave the house? Was this a sudden decision?
PATIENT: I do not like to have people stare at me, so I decided to stay home.

[At this juncture the dialogue could take a bad direction. An important element is to take the patient's assumption as the starting point and not question it in any way. The doctor does not ask, "Do people stare at you?" or "Do you think that they were staring at you?" These would clearly show disbelief of the patient's assumptions. Instead, the doctor accepts the patient's assumptions, asking, "Why did people stare at you?" The patient may then become acutely uncomfortable because he does not know. The doctor then moves closer to reality.]

DOCTOR: Were they acquaintances or strangers?
PATIENT: I don't know.

[This is another turning point in the conversation because the doctor can say with all sincerity, "I can see no reason why people should stare at you." In this instance, the patient can either show relief or become suspicious of the doctor. It is possible that many people have tried to reason with him in just this manner and because he was suspicious of them, he may become suspicious of the doctor.]

PATIENT: People stare at me because I am so ugly.

[This time, instead of agreeing or disagreeing with the patient's frame of reference by saying that he finds him attractive or unattractive in appearance, the doctor tries not to interject his own personal idea of beauty, which is irrelevant in the interview, but continues on to try to uncover the patient's view of his appearance, to learn what he considers elements of ugliness. It might merely be that the patient has a recent scar or accident or has had a deformity from childhood that has given him a particular point of view about ugliness. If a line of inquiry is thwarted by the patient, the doctor can react in a very human way by showing irritation. If he is forced to change the mode of inquiry, he will show the patient the reason for the change—for example, that the patient is forcing him into that particular mode. Through all of this, the doctor is careful not to create anxiety in the patient, but tries to show him that the doctor too is human.]

The use of this dialogue is an attempt to show the reader the type of approach that Sullivan has brought to psychiatry, the elements of concern that he has noted.

When he died, in 1949, Sullivan was one of the most influential American psychiatrists. His work extended the insights of psychiatry into the field of social science by dealing with actual relationships between people. His influence is still strongly felt today through his writings and collections of his lectures which his colleagues and disciples have published.

Instead of meta-talk Sullivan used the term "verbalisms" to describe the statements and expressions that hold hidden meanings. He wrote of one such verbalism, "In a very long psychiatric career I would say that I have come to have more and more affection for the rationalization which ends with 'just because'; the more words that follow, the harder it is to figure out how much is personal verbalism, rationalization, as it is called, and how much is an important clue to something that one ought to see." He believed that each of us has a growing ability to conceal and deceive through the use of verbalisms which tend to fall into patterns of appropriate and inappropriate behavior. By the time a child reaches the age of 10, he has become quite adept at concealing feelings that might bring on reprisals. As a result, he becomes expert in using phrases or expressions that hide his real intentions and inquiries. The child may ask his parents perfectly rational questions regarding their behavior while his meta-talk is expressing concern about why they are always so unhappy or angry with each other in the early morning. Sullivan observes that "in an attempt to catch on to something which is understandable, the child begins to ask questions that are beside the point. Now, they aren't beside the point to the child, but the anxiety element requires that the child shall use words to conceal what is being inquired about."

The same pattern of questions is used later in life by adults. In a situation where a wife wants to find out what her husband was really doing during his business trip, she begins by asking an innocuous question; "How was the trip?" "Where did you eat?" or "Meet anyone interesting?" Sometimes the husband, understanding the underlying meaning af the questions, quickly responds by reassuring her that every interpersonal encounter was strictly business.

Once she is satisfied, she ceases the veiled questioning, and all is serene in their relationship.

Sullivan also touched on another very important aspect of meta-talk which he called "prejudicial verbalisms." These were described as the result of "selective inattention," or as others have called it, "selective perception." He believed that "we fail to recognize the actual import of a good many things we see, hear, think, do and say, not because there is anything the matter with our zones of interaction with others but because the process of inferential analysis is opposed by the self-system." The meta-talk in phrases such as "I know—I know," "From my point of view," and "Based on my experience" are typical of such selective inattention. The expression "The wife is the last person to know" could illustrate that in order to maintain her self-esteem, the wife will only "see" the evidence which affirms her established social position.

Sullivan mentions a couple which "makes what certainly is a marriage of great convenience. Friends of each notice with increasing discomfort that husband and wife seem more and more bent on humiliating each other in the presence of friends." The meta-talk one might hear at a social gathering with them would be loaded with hidden sarcasm and loathing. Sometimes, less observant persons hear this meta-talk and interpret it as kidding or playful behavior. Before making that assumption, one might do well to observe the congruent gestures. If someone says, "You always say silly things like that!" and crosses her arms, or raises an eyebrow, "silly" may mean "stupid." If, on the other hand, the speaker smiles at the listener and touches him lightly as she moves toward him, silly may mean "very clever," intended as a compliment rather than a derogatory remark.

Sullivan states, "Everyone of us in our early formation years—perhaps all through childhood, and certainly later in the juvenile period—had opportunities to learn that certain combinations of words and gestures would minimize, if not remove, the danger of anxiety." People do develop set patterns of negotiating in early childhood. These were established to deal with anxiety-producing situations. Once used successfully, they tend to be perpetuated and form permanent life-styles. Our belief is that these life-styles should always be open and subject to change depending on new life experience.

Sandor Feldman

In his work *Mannerisms of Speech and Gestures in Everyday Life*, Dr. Sandor Feldman, a clinical psychiatrist, presented the results of observations made during interpersonal communication with his patients and also nonpatients whom he met socially. From these encounters he concluded that persons often consciously or unconsciously conceal what they truly want to say by the use of what we call meta-talk. The work by Feldman, originally published in 1959, should have triggered many studies in the field. However, very little additional material has been published in the intervening years.

Feldman uses "by the way" as an example of personal censorship combined with an overwhelming drive to say something significant. He even chided the great Sigmund Freud for using the expression, noting that Freud used it in writing about a patient: "The analysis—which, by the way, led to a cure—revealed . . . ," motivated Dr. Feldman to ask, "I wonder whether Freud used 'by the way' in a legitimate way. He could conceivably have done so had the passage concerned itself with the process of therapy. But how could he have been using this phrase legitimately when the passage has nothing to do with therapy?"

Dr. Feldman's conclusions parallel ours with regard to other expressions, such as "incidentally" and "before I forget" that are used to hide or minimize the importance of what is to follow. He also considers statements beginning with the words "honestly," "sincerely," or "frankly." The use of these words as an introduction to what one is about to say has overwhelmingly been interpreted in our seminars as meaning, *Watch out!* He isn't going to be honest, sincere or frank. In a negotiating situation when a person says, "Frankly, I think our demands are not excessive," he means, "I think they are, but will try to get them anyway." You may recall from your own experience, situations where these expressions caused you to disbelieve what was being said, but if the "honestly" or "frankly" had not been used, you might not have been as suspicious. Despite this general awareness, some still continue to preface their conversations with such misleading words.

The understanding of how a person uses words in meta-talk affords an important opportunity for unraveling the mental activity of that person. However, do not jump to fast conclusions. Carefully study clusters of phrases and gestures to be sure the meta-messages are consistently presented. For example, take "I'd like to talk to you," uttered by a lady who then touches you lightly as she leans toward you, as opposed to the man who says the same thing while crossing his arms, turning his body away, and looking down his nose at you. Completely opposite meanings have been communicated. The first says, "I care for you and want to share with you"; the second, "You'd better be careful!"

iv

SOME PAST AND PRESENT
IDEAS ABOUT TALK

ARISTOTELIAN RHETORIC

Throughout recorded history men have attempted to find techniques and methods for bringing fellow human beings under the control of their will. Rhetoric was one of the first attempts to reach this goal by a formalized process. Significantly, rhetoric was developed in city-states of ancient Greece, where instead of persuading one man—the king or the tyrant—large bodies of the citizenry had to be moved to support a certain course of action. The most famous of the ancient authorities on rhetoric was Aristotle, the great classifier and assigner of categories. Structuring rhetoric, as he did all of his studies of theoretical and practical philosophies, he applied his "true" principles of human life to rhetoric and devised a static system of essential properties. Unfortunately, most

66

subsequent studies dealt with Aristotle's classifications as finalities rather than as starting points from which to consider today's open-ended life processes. Thus the study of classical rhetoric has fallen into disuse, not because Aristotle's ideas were followed but rather because his broad guidance and necessary cautions were ignored.

Aristotle stated that the elements of rhetoric—persuasion, public speaking, and logical discussion—should be dealt with and studied systematically. Rhetoric itself he regarded as an art. It has often been said that Aristotle was only concerned with methods of persuasion. "Rhetorical study in its strict sense is concerned with modes of persuasion" is frequently cited as "proving" this point of view. This ignores Aristotle's strong ethical concern revealed in his words: "It may also be noted that man has a sufficient natural instinct for what is true and usually does arrive at the truth. Hence the man who makes a good guess at truth is likely to make a good guess at probabilities." Ethical considerations were paramount when he said, "Rhetoric is useful because things that are true and things that are just have a natural tendency to prevail over their opposites." And, "Things that are true and things that are better are, by their nature, practically always easier to prove and easier to believe in." However, he seems aware of possible misunderstanding when he observes: "And if it be objected that one who uses such power of speech unjustly might do great harm, that is a charge which may be made in common against all good things except virtue . . . It is clear, further, that its function is not simply to succeed in persuading, but rather to discover the means of coming as near such success as the circumstances of each particular case allow." It seems obvious from this that Aristotle uses the term "success" in its moral as well as its practical sense for he immediately reminds us of the broader meaning: "In rhetoric, however, the term 'rhetorician' may describe either the speaker's knowledge of the art, or his moral purpose." Moral purpose, to Aristotle, was of as great concern as knowledge of the art.

Those today who regard rhetoricians as craftsmen of persuasion, who consider rhetoric as a mere technique for proving one's point—or seeming to—or for creating an impression on an audience, are describing a body of knowledge without a spirit. Rhetoric cannot be separated from its purposes, and, as Isocrates observed, the true advantage of the rhetorician is moral superiority. This advantage is much needed today by individuals, groups, and, indeed, all mankind. As more and more people return to the ideas of Aristotle the innovator, and set new directions for the uses and goals of motivation, fertile ground is being broken and planted. General semantics and other new disciplines are harvesting the fruit. The art of negotiating is but one of benefits of the new rhetoric, a tool that can help us meet the difficult and complex problems of today with skill and precision.

BENTHAM'S LINGUISTIC STUDIES

Political rhetoric, as practiced in the late eighteenth century, held little charm for the English philosopher Jeremy Bentham. He wrote a lengthy and harsh indictment of oratorical practices (from *A Bentham Reader*, Mary Peter Mack, ed.) calling them:

> a perpetual vein of nonsense, flowing from a perpetual abuse of words—words having a variety of meanings, where words with single meanings were equally at

hand; the same words used in a variety of meanings in the same page; words used in meanings not their own, where proper words were equally at hand; words and propositions of the most unbounded signification, turned loose without any of those exceptions or modifications which are so necessary on every occasion to reduce their import within the compass, not only of right reason, but even of the design in hand, of whatever nature it may be: the same inaccuracy, the same inattention in the penning of this cluster of truths, on which the fate of nations was to hang, as if it had been an oriental tale, or an allegory for a magazine: stale epigrams, instead of necessary distinctions; figurative expressions preferred to simple ones; sentimental conceits as trite as they are unmeaning, preferred to apt and precise expressions; frippery ornament preferred to the majestic simplicity of good sound sense; and the acts of the senate loaded and disfigured by the tinsel of the playhouse.

His admonitions are still important today in our attempts to understand effective communication. The great trouble, Bentham thought, was the use of "fictions . . . saying something exists which does not exist, and acting as if it existed." "By a real entity, understand a substance—an object, the existence of which is made known to us by one or more of our five senses . . . By a fictitious entity, understand an object, the existence of which is feigned by the imagination—feigned for the purpose of discourse—and which, when so formed is spoken of as a real one." The probability range he used was as follows: fact (certain), hypothesis (probable), theory (possible), and fiction (impossible). However, Bentham did not advocate the abolition of fictions in discourse. That "would be as much as to say that no discourse in the subject of which the operations, or affections, or other phenomena of the mind are included, ought ever to be held." When fictions are used, however, their use should be made known to the listener so that he can "perceive and understand the use and value, as well as the nature of the instruction communicated to him."

Another difficulty in communication is that "what we are continually talking of, merely from our having been continually talking of it, we imagine we understand; so close a union has habit connected between words and things, that we take one for the other. . . ." There are two solutions to this problem, either "lay aside the old phraseology and invent a new one," or "enter into a long discussion, to state the whole matter at large. . . ." A less painful alternative is to purge words and phrases of their "adventitious and unsuitable ideas" by using neutral expressions. "Thus, instead of the word *lust*, by putting together two words in common use . . . frame the neutral expression, *sexual desire*. . . ." Or, instead of *avarice*, one could use *pecuniary interest*.

Bentham himself told of a childhood filled with terror of the dark because of talk of ghosts and demons the servants tormented him with. Ever afterwards, he compensated for this fear by seeking clarity in all things, most importantly in communication with others.

General Semantics

A study that offers, among other things, insights into the nature of man's linguistic behavior is general semantics. It was formulated by Count Alfred Korzybski, whose major work, *Science and Sanity*, defines the subject as follows: "General semantics is not any 'philosophy' or 'psychology' or 'logic' in the ordinary sense. It is a new extensional discipline which explains and trains us how to use our nervous system most efficiently." The adjective "general" was added to avoid confusion with other logical and linguistic studies referred to as "semantics."

Our day-to-day use of evaluative thought has not kept up with methods used in the formulation of modern science. A corrective approach is suggested in *Science and Sanity*: "The structure of the world is, in principle, unknown; and the only aim of knowledge and science is to discover this structure. The structure of language is potentially known, if we pay attention to it. Our only possible procedure in advancing our knowledge is to match our verbal structures, often called theories, with empirical structures, and see if our verbal predictions are fulfilled empirically or not, thus indicating that the two structures are either similar or dissimilar." Stated differently: We should be aware of our language habits and change them to make our verbal predictions conform as closely as possible to the outside world of empirical happenings.

Modern science has shown that our ordinary language has led to an oversimplification of our concepts of reality. Among other difficulties this causes, we tend to confuse our words with the things they represent, we do not realize the limits of our abstractions (words, symbols), and we allow ourselves to be triggered into uncontrolled responses by these symbols.

Besides making us aware of these problems, general semantics offers practical methods and devices for improving our evaluative habits. The following list of general semantic devices is intended to increase our awareness so that when we use ordinary language it will be in conformity with up-to-date scientific knowledge of the outside world.

DEVICES	EXAMPLES OF TALK
1. Indexing (to show the uniqueness of everything in the world)	Problems in understanding talk have led to misunderstandings. Talk between parent and child and talks between nations require different considerations.
2. Dating (to show process, changing world)	The rhetoric of Aristotle is not the rhetoric of the nineteenth century nor the rhetoric of today.
3. Etc. (to avoid thinking we have considered all)	Understanding talk is useful in the home, in business, in sports, in social events, etc.
4. Hyphen (to show relatedness)	Talking is an emotional-intellectual process.
5. Quotation marks (for attention to the word)	Whenever I talk he listens quite "emotionally."
6. Circularity (relatedness of everything)	When we start talking, we can never know where it will end.
7. Extensional device (to relate to the outside world)	I said I could prove there are bugs in this room. That (pointing) is the proof.
8. Quantifying terms (for degrees)	Exactly to what extent am I committed if I say yes?
9. Abstracting (We make our own abstractions)	I tell it as it seems to me.

10. Self-reflexiveness (we use language to speak about language)

We can talk about talk.

11. Multiordinality (Meanings of words change according to the verbal level on which they are used)

Sex has different meanings for the infant, teen-ager and adult.

Etc.

V

CATEGORIES OF TALK AND THEIR DEGREE OF RELIABILITY

> "There's no use trying," [Alice] said, "one can't believe impossible things."
>
> "I dare say you haven't had much practice," said the Queen. "When I was your age, I always did it for half an hour a day. Why, sometimes I've believed as many as six impossible things before breakfast."
>
> —LEWIS CARROLL

If someone were to say, "Yes, that's true, except most of the time," or, "If I had to choose between them I'd choose them both," you would immediately recognize that you cannot act upon these statements. Probably everyone would agree with you. Basically, most people in listening to others tend to interpret the talk that they hear in a similar manner. There is, however, a hierarchy of categories in which some types of talk are more reliable and others less so. Similar hierarchies have been recognized in other fields, but none of them has previously been applied to talk.

To understand that there are categories of talk is not sufficient. You must be able to place the talk that you listen to in its appropriate category so that you can understand what is being offered to you or hidden from you simply by recognizing the category of the speaker's talk.

The following categories are arranged in an approximate order of increasing reliability:

A. Group prejudgment
B. Insufficient information
C. Stereotyped information
D. Personal information
E. Systematically arranged information
F. Meaningful information
G. Information of proven relevance

Group Prejudgment

> "It is not disbelief that is dangerous to our society; it is belief."
>
> —GEORGE BERNARD SHAW

"What do you expect of their kind?" is a generalization based upon limited experience. Perhaps the speaker's experience with "their kind" has been with three or four people of "their kind" and in each case it has been an unfortunate experience. Since blatant misbehavior is far more likely to attract attention than unobtrusive goodness, the quota of three or four can be easily and rapidly filled. Unfortunately, this judgment of a few now extends to all members of "their kind" and all future attempts at communication between the speaker and "them" will be seriously impaired. As for the degree of reliability of statements on "their kind," it would be as unreliable as a scientist basing a theory on the results of a single experiment. As the old saying goes, "An example is no proof."

Insufficient Information—
Don't Confuse Me with the Facts,
I've Already Made Up My Mind

"The art of reading is to skip judiciously."
—PHILIP G. HAMERTON

Many hundreds of years ago, a group of learned Greeks met together to decide how many teeth were in a woman's mouth. Rather than merely looking and counting, they discussed it on the basis of size and shape of the jaw and the relative size of women. Obviously since women have smaller bodies and jaws than men, they must also have fewer teeth.

The following story illustrates how a person can be under-informed when he simply relies on the apparent reply: A man went into a restaurant and ordered a turkey sandwich. The waitress said, "I'm sorry, but we're out of turkey." "Well then, I'll have a chicken sandwich." The waitress then said, "If I had chicken, don't you think I would have given you a turkey sandwich?"

Stereotyped Information—
The Candidate Is a Liberal-Radical-
Conservative

"Unfounded beliefs are the homage which impulse pays to reason."
—BERTRAND RUSSELL

A person who makes use of stereotypes deals with life in an egg-crate fashion. He divides the world into small segments, each one self-contained. For him, nothing on a particular subject can take place outside the rigid boundaries he has drawn for it. His talk patterns confirm and reinforce these categories. A politician can only be a liberal or a radical or a conservative. But if he is thoroughly upset with a special breed, he might call the politician a liberal-radical-conservative to touch all the stereotype bases.

Before World War II, in America, "Made in Japan" was a stereotype for imitation, second-rate. To later generations it has meant superior design and equipment in electronics and photography. But that too is a stereotype. Another example of stereotyped thinking is the exchange between President Woodrow Wilson and French Premier Georges Clemenceau at the Paris Peace Conference at the end of World War I. Wilson: "But don't you believe in the brotherhood of man?" Clemenceau: "Yes, I believe in the brotherhood of man. Cain and Abel! Cain and Abel!"

Personal Information

> "People are usually more convinced by reasons they discovered themselves than by those found by others."
> —BLAISE PASCAL

"Based on what I know of him, I'd say he's guilty." A statement of this sort would never get a person in the jury box, but it has some degree of reliability because it is based on personal experience and/or prejudice. Baron Rothschild, hosting at a formal dinner, dismissed the matter of who should sit where by the following personal observation: "Those that matter won't mind where they sit and those that mind don't matter."

Systematically Arranged Information— It's as Simple as 1 + 1 = 2

". . . to make judgment wholly by their rules is the humor of a scholar."

· —FRANCIS BACON

"The most fluent talkers or most plausible reasoners are not always the justest thinkers."

—WILLIAM HAZLITT

A considerable number of people place great reliance on the systematic approach. There is nothing basically wrong with relying on one or more systematic approaches, but one should realize the limitations of each. A systematic approach is only one method of covering a broad life experience. When someone says, "It's as simple as 1 + 1 = 2," we should realize that this applies only to the digital system. In the binary system, 1 and 1 is written 10, and in the dozen system, 1 dozen and 1 dozen equals 24. So if we plan to rely on systematic approaches, we should recognize that they work fairly well, but only within the areas for which they were designed. Euclidean geometry worked well when dealing with small areas on supposedly flat surfaces. But when dealing with the real world and curved surfaces, non-Euclidean geometry was essential. Noam Chomsky is supposed to have said that no language is structured so that a sentence has a negative meaning when the words are reversed. To which a student replied, "It does. Does it?" This reveals a systematic concept which is not all-inclusive.

Meaningful Information—
The Whole Is Greater than the
Sum of the Parts

"What is the answer?" Gertrude Stein asked on her deathbed. Then, when there was a silence, she asked: "In that case, what is the question?"

"Anybody can become angry—that is easy; but to be angry with the right person, and in the right degree, and at the right time, and for the right purpose, and in the right way—that is not within everybody's power and it is not easy."

—ARISTOTLE

Many of the facts that we accept and use are based upon what we believe in and what we believe everyone *should* believe in. They have become meaningful to us because they have been confirmed time and time again in our life experiences. Of course, this does not mean that all men will agree with our judgments. We may say that all men are inherently good, while others say they are evil. Each side would have its followers. But our primary consideration is that of communication. A person of strong moral convictions is more likely to provide you with reliable information about what he really means than the person who relies on stereotypes. In most instances he says what he feels and thinks. And human nature is such that the reaction to that person is more likely to be admiration and respect rather than disagreement with even the most quixotic belief.

Information of Proven Relevance—
In Giving Love We Lose Nothing

"The shaping of the thought of students demands that
we teach them to have the proper respect and the proper
disrespect for the knowledge of our day. It demands that
we simultaneously teach students to accept and reject
dogma, and more important, to know when to accept
and when to reject. This is a demanding task to ask of
our staff, and is an even more demanding task to ask of
our students. Such a goal can only be accomplished in a
research atmosphere, and students must see with their
own eyes how useful the knowledge of our day can be,
and at the same time, and in spite of its usefulness, students must see how this selfsame knowledge is continually being destroyed, and, through research, is continually being replaced."
—Dr. Johns, President, University of Alberta

What has been proven relevant and, therefore,
workable for us, has a greater degree of reliability for us in
the future. We are prepared to act in ways that we have
found to be reliable and, therefore, believable. Of course,
nothing is absolute and nothing is absolutely reliable. It
cannot be. But, even though our most cherished beliefs may
prove in the long run to be wrong, they nonetheless have
had a greater degree of reliability for us in the past because
they have been relevant to our life experience. They also
have conveyed to the listener a greater degree of reliability
than any of the other steps in the hierarchy that we have
presented.

vi
ASSUMPTIONS

A retired captain of industry observed that when he was younger the sight of black smoke billowing from factory chimneys meant full employment to him. Now, however, it meant air pollution.

A manufacturer was awarded a contract to provide policemen with helmets for riot control. His helmet met all specifications: it was comfortable and lightweight, yet could resist the heavy impact of bricks and other objects that might be thrown. All factory tests were passed. However, the first time the helmets were used in a riot-control situation, they were found to suffer a fatal flaw—they were flammable.

A bathing-suit manufacturer advertised extensively in trade papers that he would hold a topless bathing-suit contest. A large number of men, many of them not in the trade, showed up. Soon after the contest began, however, the audience drifted away. The contestants were all men.

In each of these three anecdotes an assumption is made. The first deals with a conscious assumption showing that even the same set of circumstances viewed at different times can produce different conclusions. The second deals with a hidden assumption that every eventuality can be anticipated. The third is an unconscious assumption produced in others.

The following story contains several examples of assumptions.

A Hungarian refugee who had settled in the United States was informed of the death of a close relative in Hungary and decided to return to attend the funeral. Although many years had passed since the revolt that had caused him to leave, he was rather nervous as he drove a rented car across the Austrian border into his native land. He attended the funeral without incident and began the long drive back to Vienna in the middle of the night. Suddenly a rear tire blew out, he lost control of the car, and it careened into a bridge abutment. As it did so, the windshield literally exploded. Still unharmed, thinking he was being shot at, he leaped from the car—into a deep hole. He emerged with a sprained ankle and several broken ribs.

The car-rental agency immediately sent another car with a driver to take him back to Vienna. There he was referred to an outstanding orthopedist. When he arrived at the address, he was dismayed to find that he would have to climb twenty steps to reach the office. There was no elevator. He limped up the stairs, received treatment, and afterwards remarked to the doctor that it seemed odd that an orthopedist should have an office where his patients had to climb a steep flight of stairs. The doctor smiled and explained that when he had first moved into his office he had been employed by an insurance company. He had wanted to be able to testify in court that people who had claimed serious injuries had been able to mount the stairs without great difficulty.

There are at least two assumptions made in this story. The first is a hidden one that the refugee made: Hungary is still a dangerous place for me to be. The second is the unconscious assumption a judge might make upon being told that the injured party had been able to climb stairs.

Conscious Assumptions

"We sit on our assumptions."

Although hidden assumptions may lead to misinterpretations and mistakes, the conscious use of assumptions is a valuable human process. It permits us to probe the world before we subject ourselves to an actual experience. If the probe seems valid, we then commit ourselves. If not, we discard the assumption. An assumption is like a flashlight battery. As long as it is fresh, it does useful work. When it is weak or dead it must be replaced.

Diverse philosophers have offered various proofs that "concrete" facts rest on foundations of sand—on assumptions. For example, they say that the study of physics is built on the scientifically unprovable fact that we exist. A great problem in dealing with assumptions is that they can in time become such an essential part of our thinking process that they are considered immutable facts. In teaching a child to swim we sometimes must force him to give up the inflated float and chance the hostile water on his own. So it is with our assumptions which no longer serve a useful purpose. Few people learn to review their assumptions as a scientist constantly reviews his hypotheses. A hypothesis remains true only as long as it continues to meet all of life's conditions. As soon as it is found wanting, the hypothesis must be changed, not the condition that casts doubt on its validity. The assumption-making process is a great human achievement. When used with an awareness of its possible limitations, it provides the necessary alternatives for dealing with the outside world. The answers of tomorrow may be found in the as yet unrecognized hidden assumptions of today.

Hidden Assumptions

"This is the best and only way."

Although it is not difficult to recognize hidden or unconscious assumptions in others, we usually recognize our own only when we are brought up short by a life situation. Suddenly we are aware that our assumptions do not correspond to reality. General semanticists have used this fact to demonstrate the difference between assumption and reality. A lecturer would hold up a pencil, walk about the classroom, and ask his students to write down as many characteristics of the object as they could in forty seconds. After they had done so, he would ask, "Would you change any of the characteristics that you have written down if you saw me do this?" Then he would bend the "pencil" in half. It was made of rubber. Then he would explain that any of the characteristics they would change were based on their assumptions.

Some time ago during one of the lectures a student who was thoroughly familiar with the experiment wrote, "It appears to me to be yellow. It appears to me to have a point. It appears to me to be cylindrical in shape." These were accepted answers but the student could not resist adding: "I also use a rubber pencil like that in my own demonstrations." However, when the cards were collected, the lecturer dropped the "pencil." It fell on the table with a loud metallic clang. The lecturer had lost his rubber pencil and had replaced it with a steel one. The student learned anew.

Talk can provide an insight into a person's assumptions. If you know a person's assumptions you can understand his facts, follow his premises, predict his conclusions and deal with his behavior. The words we use can limit our ability to meet a continually changing world. This happens whenever we start with the assumption that "this is the best and only way." The human mind tends to go along with verbal assumptions because it can quickly and efficiently reach a solution and go on to the other problems. Thus, when we say, "This is the best and only way," there is no reason for us to think about the problem any further, even subconsciously. Suppose it were remotely possible to evaluate all of the aspects of a life situation and come up with the best answer. Would it necessarily hold true for the next day—or even the next hour? When we make such a statement even to ourselves, we stop all future thinking on the subject.

Our very language has many hidden assumptions built into it. "Sunrise" and "sunset" contain a hidden assumption that for thousands of years may have prevented man from ever considering that the earth might revolve around the sun. A mental patient demanding that his psychiatrist tell him the "truth" may actually be saying, "What have you got against me?" He makes a hidden assumption that the psychiatrist is a judge handing down a judgment in the name of the community.

Producing Unconscious Assumptions in Others

Many people, recognizing the fact that everyone makes assumptions, use this fact to manipulate others by forcing them to make unconscious assumptions. A friend casually asks a woman, "Was your husband out with his sister last night?" She knows full well that the husband has no sister and that even if he had he would not have behaved as he did with the other woman. However, she does not want the onus placed on her. Instead of saying, "Because I'm your friend, I'd like to tell you," she plants a hidden assumption in the wife's mind and almost compels her to reach a conclusion that supports her message.

This device is widely used in personal and business situations. "Of course" is often employed to introduce the assumption that the speaker wishes the listener to make. "Of course, I wouldn't hold you to those terms" all too often means, "Yes I would." "Of course" can also be ambiguous and can be used to let the other person make any hidden assumption. Is the husband who responds with "Of course" to his wife's question "Do you still love me?" really saying, "Yes, I do" or "No, I don't"? The wife, however, has revealed a hidden assumption: that he once did love her, which may or may not be true.

Recently, the owner of a striking professional baseball team said, "Of course, the players can work out on their own." What did he mean? That he allowed them to? Wouldn't stop them? Or, expected them to do so? Does the husband who says of his wife's visits to their doctor, "Of course, he looks at his nude women patients with a purely professional eye" mean that the doctor is not sexually excited by his wife or that she is safe with him?

Sometimes unconscious assumptions create an odd negotiating situation in which the questions uppermost in the opposition's minds are never brought to the verbal level. For example, a buyer needs delivery of merchandise from a sole supplier by a certain date. He assumes that if he asks the supplier for a definite commitment, he will say, "No, there is some question as to whether we can." The supplier may not want to discuss a date because, although they are going to try to deliver on time, they are not absolutely sure they can do it. Neither party, therefore, will discuss a date, and both can go on to the further assumption that the matter is settled between them. If their assumptions prove to be wrong, there are likely to be recriminations and bad feelings between them. Unless an ambiguous solution is your goal, try to share assumptions. State fully and frankly what is on your mind and attempt to find out what is on your opposer's mind. Of course, if the unresolved problem never arises, both parties can remain happy with their assumptions.

vii
RELATIONSHIPS

"To be is to be related."
—Cassius J. Keyser

Through reasoning we impose a system of relationships on a constantly changing world. Once a common element or thread is indicated, we acknowledge this by using words to define the relationship that has been revealed. In other words, we give labels to our relationships. To illustrate the different relationships we make, place ten to twenty different items on a table top, then make a list of the many relationships that you can discover that exist between these supposedly independent objects. The list can be almost endless, e.g., how they are placed, what they are made of, how old they are, the many different categories that we might assign to them, etcetera.

Words, in addition to designating a relationship (as in husband and wife, parent and child, and so forth), may also define a formal compact between two or more parties. An oath of office creates a new relationship between a man and society at large. He is no longer Thomas Jones, lawyer, let us say, but mayor of the city or president of the country. This new title becomes more meaningful than "Mr. Jones" because it implies the change in relationship between Jones and society. He now has certain duties, obligations, and perquisites as defined by the oath and assumed on the basis of precedents. More informal initiations of changes in relationships take place in business and industry, but they are no less significant to the organization or the man who has been promoted (or demoted). And the meta-talk between the man and his colleagues also changes when the relationship changes.

A similar change takes place when Mr. Smith and Miss Perkins are told, "I now pronounce you man and wife." Not only has Miss Perkins become Mrs. Smith but she is now "wife" with all that the term implies in the society in which they live. Mr. Smith retains his name but he is now "husband," a term that has certain liabilities and assets which society imposes on it. Both husband and wife are bound by their preconceptions of how "marriage" is to be defined and conducted.

In all of this, there is one grave danger. The participants in the establishment of a relationship have hidden assumptions about it. They "know" how they will act and how others should act. No one is ever completely prepared or unprepared for a change. When Victoria became Queen, she was 18 years old. She had been isolated from all outside influence by her mother and her mother's unscrupulous lover, but within hours of her uncle the king's death she presided over a cabinet meeting "acting every inch a queen." (In this instance the cliché may have been apt.) But in her preparation for the moment when she would assume the crown, Victoria had made many assumptions, among them that she could be an autocrat and (a hidden one) that the British people would put up with it. Neither was correct.

Unfortunately, we all make hidden assumptions about our relationships, in fact we often make stereotyped clichés of them. They are assigned rigid forms and customs that must never seem to change. Even people who realize that everything in life changes, and that they personally must always be willing to adapt to change, refuse to recognize that relationships, certainly a most important part of life, must change too. We should keep our evaluation open in the standards we ascribe to relationships.

Dr. Haim Ginott, psychologist, writer, and teacher, in "The Psychotherapist as Parent," discusses a relationship in which "The public expects its mental health expert to be a better parent. If he personally cannot benefit from his professional experience and insight, what hope is there for his patients?" Yet in the dialogue between two child psychotherapists in which the article is framed, one observes, "I, for instance, deal with my son essentially the way my mother dealt with me. I sometimes even use her tone of voice. It is as though I were replaying a familiar tape." How unfortunate that even our professionals have permitted their roles in life to become frozen.

Relationships are damaged, sometimes irreparably, by the assumption that what has once worked in the past will work again today. That can happen, but more often it is at the expense of undermining the present relationship. Take the situation of the alcoholic husband and the forgiving wife as an example. Both are bound to an essentially deteriorating relationship in which the cliché, "I'll never take another drink," and its acceptance by the wife, mark the boundaries of a situation in which there is little hope of change for the better. It becomes a diminishing cycle of alcoholism, recrimination, and forgiveness. It is like the mythological bird that flew in ever-decreasing concentric circles until it finally disappeared within itself.

How does one "take the pulse" of a relationship to see if it is viable? One way is to observe objectively if patterns of behavior and talk have disintegrated into clichés. Another is to make use of the concept of immediacy to determine the closeness or distance between the partners. The relationship should also be judged on a higher level: whether or not it relates constructively to the outside world. After all, "It's them against us" indicates a close relationship but scarcely a constructive one. "Like two peas in a pod" is a little better but probably describes a relationship that is too bland to be creative. To describe a truly effective relationship we would have to turn away from clichés and use words that describe a conscious oneness, a close, dynamic participation between people and their world.

One of the most famous examples of a successful relationship is contained in the Declaration of Independence. Consider the following passage: "And for the support of this Declaration, with a firm Reliance on the Protection of divine Providence, we mutually pledge to each other our Lives, our Fortunes and our sacred Honor." The words themselves virtually direct success for a joint venture. They also illustrate the risk of living as circumstances demand it.

Let us turn now to less grandiose words that define and sometimes limit the success of typical everyday relationships.

HUSBAND AND WIFE RELATIONSHIP

"Married couples who love each other tell each other
thousands of things without talking."
—CHINESE PROVERB

Most marriages are started by a romantic fire.
This first brush with love is certainly more exciting than the
routine involvement in marriage. Some flames last long
enough to permit the parties to adjust to each other's faults.
This is understandable—marriage brings together for life
two people who scarcely know one another.

Marriage is one long conversation, hopefully seasoned
with understanding. This helps overcome the punctuation
of disputes. The spouse who listens to one word and hears
two, and knows the many things conveyed without talk has
the basic ingredients for understanding.

Unfortunately, even today if one of the parties in a
marriage is an important world celebrity, he or she has little
idea of what the other party thinks of him or her.

All that has been said about the marriage relationship has
frightened many members of the younger generation. This
fear can be related to the story about an airline stewardess
who says, "Fasten your seat belt. It will be less dangerous."
In the passenger's mind, seat belts and danger are equated
as a result of this statement. Another hostess might say,
"Fasten your seat belts. It will make you more comfortable."
In this way the reaction of seat belts and danger is taken
away completely and is replaced with seat belts and comfort.

The hidden dangers in any life experience should not
discourage young people from trying. A marriage, for ex-

ample, could be considered, as the second stewardess implied, an exercise in degrees of comfort.

Successful marriages permit a constant flow of information and understanding between the partners. Marriages based merely on hidden assumptions and clichés are likely to be less successful. There is communication in these marriages but it consists of abrupt stops and starts: a message is given, it is received, and then taken as a rebuff. Even attempts that would appear to be seeking understanding are abandoned. When one of the partners makes a fresh, tentative new approach and the response is, "We'll see" or "I'll think about it" [DELAYER], the other assumes it to mean, "Don't bother me" or "Let's put it off until you forget about it."

The same clichés are usually used over and over again, sometimes with slight variations. An example is the husband working for hours on a major project. He wants to try to finish the job. His wife, perhaps with the best intentions, is concerned that he is too tense and needs to relax or is afraid that the dinner will be ruined. She may start with: "What time will you be ready for dinner?" and is answered with a preoccupied, "Just a minute" [DELAYER]. "Dinner is almost ready" brings an "I'll be right there" [DELAYER]. "Dinner's ready" prompts, "It'll be just a few more minutes" [DELAYER]. Here or soon afterward an explosion takes place. The husband may say, "Honey, please, I'm trying to finish this!" The wife may threaten mayhem or just let the dinner burn. This could have been avoided if at the start the husband with understanding had asked, "What time do you want to have dinner?" A direct flow of information would not have been interrupted by cliché questions and answers and a better mutual relationship would develop.

However, one man's thoughtful question may be another man's cliché. Many an irritated wife can tell you that an oft-repeated "What time do you want to have dinner?" may mean, "I'm hungry. Why don't we eat *now?*"

In most marriages, there is constant meta-talk which seeks reassurance, expresses suspicion, denies involvement with a third party, and in general seeks to reestablish an equilibrium in the relationship. Sometimes one's meta-talk appears quite blunt, as when the husband expresses enthusiasm for another woman's physical charms. However, such a statement has many nuances and must be considered with the gestures, tone, volume of voice, and other signs. A view of the total picture may reveal a secure relationship, an attempt to create jealousy, or something in between. The more damaging type of remark is usually a cliché ("Boy, is she built!"). That intentionally may provoke another cliché ("You never say anything nice about *me*"). Some husbands attempt to minimize their interest in the lady by saying "I was *only* looking at her dress" [CONVINCER].

Immediacy and distance contained in the statement can also indicate the degree of involvement: "I'm out here talking with Edith" (a pleasant innocent situation); "I'm out here talking to Edith" (and keeping her at arm's length); "I've been out here talking to Edith" (defensive); "Should we go out and talk to Edith?" (cooperative social obligation); "Let's go talk with Edith!" (a pleasant, mutual pastime); "You talk to Edith" (hostility, noninvolvement); "They always talk to Edith" (disapproval of both parties).

Sometimes a wife, not wanting to show jealousy, will construct a daisy chain of cliché inquiries. If the husband is not aware of the direction the meta-talk is taking, he may find himself inadvertently cornered. A sample might be innocently addressed over breakfast to a husband who has stayed out too late on his poker night: "Where did you go last night?"; "What did you have to eat?"; "Did you all enjoy it?"; "Who was with you?" [INTERESTERS]. If the husband is alert to this meta-talk, he will be able to tell his spouse he was a winner and couldn't leave earlier and that he loves her. He thereby successfully avoids adding a dramatic chapter to his marriage.

Money can be given an exaggerated role in the cliché-ridden marriage. "Money is more important to you than I am" [CONVINCER], or "You only married me for my money," can be destructive self-fulfilling prophecies. Where both parties are working: "Can you afford it?" disregards the husband and wife as a unit, as does "I'd like to go to a really nice place this year," "You aren't even trying to save money," "I wouldn't have bought that," "What did you buy that for?" [JUDGERS]. All of these signal a superior-inferior relationship, ostensibly based on a higher and lower income, but really indicating a relationship dominated merely by self-interest. Unless there can be degrees of mutual sharing, the partnership potential never arises.

Most people enter a marriage with a stock of standard clichés. A husband can help overcome the initial period by working with his new wife's attempts at economy when she says, "It only costs fifty dollars" or "It was reduced and I saved twenty dollars" [CONVINCERS]. The wife, in turn, can respond with sympathy when her husband rationalizes, "I didn't want that promotion. We would have had to move" [CONVINCER]. The help that each can give to the other will insure continual growth and a strong union.

Boredom and repetition can be a menace to any relationship, particularly marriage. As the then Mayor of New York Lindsay said when he spoke at a dinner after a group of stars had performed, "I feel like Zsa Zsa Gabor's fifth husband. I know how to do it, but I don't know how to make it interesting." The hidden assumption here is that the other husbands were that interesting, a judgment which Miss Gabor and others might dispute. There is also an assumption that life must always be "interesting" (meaning novel) in order to be enjoyable. Many people find fulfillment in the simple routines of daily life and look forward to performing them. Harry Truman's daily morning walk comes to mind; the ordinary things obviously gave him a great deal of pleasure. But for some people, any routine is dull. Only activities that are new and "interesting" are to be sought. They view routine in their daily lives as a small boy views the routine of having to take a bath—to be avoided by any means. There are clichés that signal this type of person: "Why can't we do something different for a change?" "Do we have to do that again?" [PERSUADERS].

One reason the question "Why can't we . . . ?" fails is that it is expressed negatively and assumes a rejection. When expressed positively and as a cooperative activity, "Let's do something different tonight" [PERSUADER], the thought has much more chance of being accepted. The same principle applies to other negatively expressed thoughts. One sure way of avoiding another person is to ask him "Why don't we get together sometime?" [DOWNER]. Not only is it negatively expressed—"sometime" places it in the distant future. Almost as effective is, "Let's get together sometime" [DOWNER]. The distance between speaker and listener is obvious.

Many devices are used to show likes and dislikes. Likes are commonly expressed in simple statements of fact: "Gee, that was good" [STROKER]. Dislikes are more covertly expressed by subtle indications of distance. A wife, let us say, asks her husband how he liked a new dish. His reply quite precisely indicates how he feels: "Delicious. Make it again soon"; "Everything was good"; "I've always liked everything you make"; "I thought it was a very good dish"; "The cheesecake and that were the best part of the meal" [STROKERS]. Less precisely: "Your meals always look so good"; "Did you get the recipe from your mother?" [DOWNERS].

Meta-talk consideration and understanding can add new dimensions to any marriage relationship.

PARENT AND CHILD RELATIONSHIP

"Mothers are fonder of their children. For they have a more painful share in their production and they are more certain that they are their own."

—ARISTOTLE

The relationship between parents and children is virtually unique in that neither party has even a semblance of free choice in deciding on a partner. If the association develops poorly, parental servitude can be worse than penal. Many a child is doomed to living the unlived life of the parent. Communication between parent and child is a subject that has preoccupied parents and academicians for centuries. Each society and each era has had its "only" way of handling communication between them. They range from virtually no communication at all to an undue familiarity. Dr. Jerome Kagan, a professor of human development at Harvard, for example, has studied Guatemalan children in remote rural villages. By custom they remain in their huts at all times for at least a year after birth; they have no toys; and their mothers rarely talk or play with them. They emerge from this experience severely retarded. (However, by the time they are eleven or twelve the village children are active, alert, and seemingly intelligent. Presumably other relationships have provided the stimulus that they needed.)

Another type of communication between children and parents is often regarded as old-fashioned but is still quite common: the parent *tells* the child. The authoritarian cliché "And no backtalk!" characterizes this type of relationship. Dr. Haim Ginott proposes the establishment of two-way communication between parent and child and observes: "Conversing with children is a unique art with rules and meanings of its own. Children are rarely naïve in their communication. Their messages are often in code that requires deciphering."

Everyone who has attempted to communicate with a child using "adult" conversation usually fails. Trying to "reason" with a child has made many a parent unreasoning. The problem is that neither is listening to the other because each is speaking a different language governed by different rules. When this fails, as it usually does, the parent resorts to clichés that threaten, accuse, attempt to praise, or try to direct: "How many times have I told you not to do that?" and other rhetorical questions are popular; "If you don't stop doing that I'll . . ." [FOREBODER] is a preface for numerous threats; "Where were you?" is as popular when used on children as adults; "You're doing a wonderful job!" has deterred many a child's desire to do anything at all; "If I were doing that I'd . . ." also turns children off; "How could you be so stupid?" [DOWNER] effectively ends all discourse. It is small wonder that, faced with these aggressive tactics, the child develops clichés of his own, as in "Where are you going?" "Out" "What are you doing?" "Nothing." The difficulties in understanding parents' roles have led to the saying that people with children and people without children feel sorry for one another.

Ginott believes that the child "wants us to understand what is going on inside himself. He wants to be understood without having to disclose what he is experiencing. It is a game in which he reveals only a little of what he feels, needing to have us guess the rest." In other words, children rely on meta-talk in their efforts to communicate. Take, for example, the child who says, "The teacher punished me." Many parents would wade in with "Why did teacher punish you?" The child isn't interested in providing that kind of information, and so he replies, "I don't know." His meta-talk is, "Don't ask me why I was punished or what I did. Instead, think of how I felt when I was disciplined in front of my classmates."

When parents say one thing and mean another they can create great anxiety and conflict in their children. Sometimes the contrast is presented verbally as when a doting mother says, "Johnny, how many times have I told you not to do that!" then turns to a friend and says, "Isn't he cute?" It is very seldom that we discover parents whose actions are an example of their maxims. But more often, the real feeling is presented nonverbally as when a busy mother says to a crying child, "Come to Mother," while her facial expression and gestures say, "Go away. Don't bother me." As we have pointed out in How to Read a Person Like a Book, children are quite aware of nonverbal communications. Anthropologist Gregory Bateson refers to this as a "double bind." After all, this was the way they sensed what their mothers meant during the time before they learned to talk. Dr. Beulah Parker in A Mingled Yarn points out that parents are usually unaware of any variance between their spoken words and their simultaneous nonverbal messages.

One consequence is the confusion in children's minds created by "masked authoritarianism." The trait is found most often in middle-class liberals whose parents were authoritarian. They tell their children they must make their own decisions but say nonverbally that it had better be a choice the parent will approve of. This incongruity can be handled by the child if only "little white lies" are involved. He knows as well as the parent that what has just been said is untrue and reacts, perhaps somewhat less precociously than the boy in the celebrated *New Yorker* cartoon: "I say it's spinach, and I say the hell with it." But in more serious instances the child is faced with either of two choices: he goes along with the parent and feels hostile or he makes up his own mind and the parent is hostile. Dr. Parker feels it is better even to resort to the authoritarian cliché "I know best." At least the child knows where he stands. Even more damaging is the parent who tries to conceal an unhappy marriage. A wife who insists to her children that all is well when they know it is not creates an incompetent feeling in them because they think they have misjudged their father.

Children, of course, are often skilled at punishing or intimidating their parents, and, one psychologist observes, "They have all the weapons." An example is the child who, realizing the parent's need for love, attempts to withdraw it with, "I don't love you anymore!" or "I hate you!" Another is, "If you don't give it to me I'll . . ." [PLEADERS]. Probably the best way to handle the situation is to treat these retorts as the clichés they are, not worthy of retaliation or worry. The child may then reevaluate his "arsenal of talk" and discard the clichés—or, if you are unlucky, he may think of more effective ones.

Possibly a course in parenthood could show how we might approach these problems with uncomplicated motivations, free interaction, mutual respect, and trust; and how we can be open to each other's emotional reactions, accept feedback, and be willing to experiment, investigate and be creative—as starters.

PARENT-TEEN-AGER RELATIONSHIP

While Alexander was a boy, Philip had great success in his affairs, at which he did not rejoice, but told the children that were brought up with him, "My father will leave me nothing to do."
—*Apophthegms of Kings and Great Commanders*

The parent, appraising the youth, says, "When I was your age I made the same mistake." The youth replies, "I'll know it is a mistake when I am your age." Can we say one is right and the other is wrong?

This situation, restated in many ways, constitutes the parent-teen-ager dilemma. Few if any other relationships are marked by such widespread lack of understanding. The adolescent's search for his own identity and independence causes him to resent any intrusion by the parent, and unfortunately most parental advice or comment on behavior is so regarded. Teen-agers are very sensitive, perhaps overly sensitive, to meta-talk that threatens to pry into their actions, endangers their life-styles, violates their privacy, and, in general, belittles their intelligence. They are often receptive to statements that sincerely convey gratitude or understanding, that encourage and are supportive of their way of life during these adolescent years.

A number of parental clichés "turn off" teen-agers ("turn off" being one of their clichés). The use of these is particularly unfortunate since suspicion of parental strategies is already a dominant element of the relationship. The parents have a need to do everything they can for their children. This includes giving advice on how to shorten the maturing process by avoiding mistakes the parent may have made or didn't make. It rarely works. As in most life experiences, things are learned by testing and experimentation. Thus, the most damaging cliché a parent can use when he attempts to relate is, "When I was your age . . ." [DOWNER]. In the first place the teen-ager doesn't believe his parents were ever "his" age. The statement also sets up the parent as an all-wise, indoctrinating, and infallible guide, a judgment the teen-ager (and every other intelligent person) knows is untrue. Finally, it places a great distance between the two— a distance of perhaps twenty years or more. In other words, this cliché not only fails to bridge the gap, it widens it. Other put-offs are rhetorical questions such as, "Why do you have to dress that way?" Again, distance is imposed, this time by obvious disapproval. (Also it feeds the teen-ager's contempt for the parent's intelligence. The answer to him is obvious: he is "doing his own thing.") "How many times do I have to tell you . . ." [JUDGER] introduces many a rhetorical question that causes instant noncommunication. The humorist Russell Baker has commented on another communication dud: "It's time you realized that one of these days you're going to have to make a living." Baker says it "stops communication, not because the adolescent resents it, but because he doesn't know what it means. He has never heard of anyone 'making a living.' He has a living, hasn't he?" Finally, there is the parent's unconditional surrender cliché, "I know I said that before!" It follows the accusation, "You already said that" [DOWNER].

But if parents use outmoded clichés, teen-agers seem gifted with coining instant clichés. This is natural. Untried and only partially experienced emotions cannot be accurately labeled by words. There is little point in listing instant clichés. As soon as adults begin to understand them (and a few trying to prove their youthfulness begin to use them), teen-agers change to new expressions that shield their inner feelings from adults. Over the past several years, however, "relevance" has been a very popular word. Adults over 30 have found to their dismay that according to their sons and daughters, they and all of their institutions and beliefs are irrelevant. This has led the iconoclastic writer Anthony Burgess to tell his college students: "I would ask you only to expand your vocabularies, develop a minimal grace of style, think harder. . . . And for God's sake stop talking about relevance. All we have is the past." Any parent could tell Mr. Burgess he is asking for a great deal more than he is likely to get.

Many rebelling teen-agers have an uncanny ability to size up their parents, know what will irritate or wound them, and use that knowledge unmercifully. A stranger would never allow this callow auditioning. If parents want information, the teen-agers talk in grunts, whistles, and clucks; if neatness, they will be sloppy; if good manners, they will violate every rule of etiquette they know.

Parents can also contribute to a communication gap with their teen-aged son or daughter by their use of meta-talk.

Immediacy or distance between a mother and a teen-ager can be illustrated by the following statements, each subsequent one indicating a somewhat greater degree of distance:

"There are clothes on the floor."
"Kindly clean up your room."
"Mother wants you to clean up the room."
"Mother wants her boy to clean up the room."

"Mother wants Johnny to clean up the room."
"Mother wants Johnny to clean up his room."
"Mother would like Johnny to clean up his room."
"Mother would like to be surprised and have Johnny clean up his room!"

Some teen-agers instinctively know how to reward their parents in excess—the story of the Midas touch. What parent would not be delighted to have a teen-ager talk frankly and openly about his life and listen with respect to the parent's comments? Let's see how this works in a letter to a newspaper advice column from a 17-year-old girl who repeats the platitudes she has received:

> I have always been honest with my parents about my activities. My friends keep theirs hidden. But my parents always try to understand. They give their opinions, which I respect though I may disagree. When I told my mother I had sexual intercourse, she felt she was a failure as a mother. My mother has given me a set of morals which I follow, in the main.

It seems as though every cliché the mother has ever uttered has been neatly fielded and tossed back to her—all for the purpose of reflecting hurt. Yet could we expect less when we mouth such clichés instead of sincerely attempting to communicate with our children. The girl uses a cliché of her own only once. This appears at the end of a series of four sentences that again illustrate how verb tense and mood can convey a sense of nearness or distance and predict what will happen in the future:

> We plan to be married in four years. I slept with my boyfriend after dating him three weeks. . . . I realize

this boy and I may separate. I will never regret our beautiful love.

This is but a vain attempt by a young woman to apply Edmund Burke's statement, "The arrogance of age must submit to be taught by youth."

PROFESSIONAL-CLIENT RELATIONSHIP

"I hold every man a debtor to his profession."
—FRANCIS BACON

The relationship between a professional and his client is unique in many ways. Only one person in the relationship, the client, usually can take the initiative in seeking out the other. The analogy can be made to the girl of yesterday, who was permitted to be available but was not permitted to take the first step in approaching a young man. The selection of a professional is basically a client's job. It is usually made on the flimsiest of criteria: availability, other people's opinions, word of mouth, blind choice, chance, and the like. True, there are a few people who have carefully evaluated their need for a lawyer, doctor, or dentist, and decided on the "best" man to handle their problem, but if they suddenly become ill or have a run-in with the law in a strange town (or even in their home town on a holiday weekend) they will probably end up taking pot luck, just as the average person does.

The client's real evaluation of the professional does not begin until they have met and there is communication between them. Here attitudes and assumptions on both sides come into play. The professional is experienced in making educated guesses based on the necessarily fragmentary data that is communicated to him ("If I may restate what you have just said . . .") [CONVINCER]. Probably he is more often right than wrong but like the client he may become a victim of hidden assumptions. In one study professional teachers in slum schools were told that certain average students had high I.Q.'s. These students did better and were given higher marks than their classmates after this "truth" had been told to the teachers. In another study "normal" researchers placed in mental hospitals were adjudged insane by the institutions' professional psychiatrists no matter how much they protested that they were sane. (Protesting actually kept them there longer.)

The client, too, may make hidden assumptions. One of the most common is that the professional is infallible— "I leave everything in your capable hands" [STROKER]. However much it might flatter the professional, this is too one-sided a relationship to be a healthy one. There must be two-way communication to achieve rewarding results. This will prevent disillusionment on the part of the client and produce a healthy skepticism on the part of the professional that he has the "only" answer. The client who suddenly discovers the professional he has consulted is not a god after all is shocked. These victims of their own delusions can be recognized by their impassioned words and statements— "shyster," "quack," "he's a butcher," "he killed my dog," "he sleeps with all his patients." Curiously, these attitudes are carried over into daily life and sometimes "professional" becomes a dirty word. A "professional politician," for example, is even more uncomplimentary than a mere "politician," and the statement "A statesman is a dead politician" shows how low in rank they already are.

Ignoring this danger, many professionals prefer to "take

charge" and want no back-talk from their clients. A defense lawyer in the Pentagon Papers case summed up this attitude in commenting on the defendants' annoying habit of having their own ideas of strategy and tactics that their attorneys opposed: "It's so much easier when you have clients that sit in the corner and let the lawyers work from there. I have a feeling when this trial is over we'll all be very happy to go our separate ways." This is an interesting use of the cliché "go our separate ways," indicating an emotional involvement with a client, albeit negative, more appropriate to a disappointed lover than a professional. The other cliché, "sit in the corner," is also revealing. Who sits in a corner? Why, a "bad boy," of course—an interesting assumption for a professional to make about his client.

There is always a risk in permitting outside emotional considerations, rather than professional intellectual competence, to rule a professional/client relationship. In the debate over the right to die with dignity, one doctor observed that, "If a physician acts to spare the family suffering and expense, he is treating society, the family's feelings, their purse, but not his patient." In effect, the patient has "lost" his doctor.

Most clients prefer the professional to show them that creative alternatives to their problems are available. Chances are they have already worried their way to the "only" solution on their own and quite often this solution is pessimistic: "You don't think they'll send me to jail, do you?"; "I guess I'll have to take a loss"; "Do you think it's malignant?"; "What about custody of the children?" [FORE-BODERS]. These and similar statements and questions are meta-talk that reveal the hidden assumptions of the client and his need for a reassuring-parent/anxious-child relationship. He wants immediate assurance that his problem is going to be taken care of. Therefore, he is particularly alert to the professional's meta-talk: "Well, George, I've heard your case and I assure you I'll do everything possible to get you off" ("Don't forget to pack your toothbrush"); "I'll do my best for you, Frank. You know that, don't you?" ("But my best is not good enough"); "I think we've caught this just in time" ("You may not die but you may wish you had") [FOREBODERS]. The client would be reassured, however, if he heard: "There are several approaches we could take to your problem." This indicates that the professional feels he can handle the problem, that he does not regard it as a stereotype, and is willing to consider all its aspects. The client is likely to respond with, "Can you help me?" ("I'm sure you can") rather than "I'm sure you are capable" ("I want someone who knows what he's talking about").

Above all, the professional should avoid trade jargon. He may impress his client who might nod his head in pretended understanding ("He'll think I'm stupid if I ask questions"). However, jargon is a one-way street. There is no opportunity for communication between individuals, one of whom needs help and the other who is paid to give it. Probably the worst offenders are professional military men. "Operation Egress Recap" sounds like an ambitious automobile tire resalvaging program. In reality, it was a program for easing the transition of Americans from prisoners of war in Indochina to free men. Mercifully, someone had the good sense to rename "Egress Recap" "Operation Homecoming." Another example: a military hospital administrator was asked how many people his cafeteria would seat. His reply was, "I do not have that statistical capability." In case you are interested, this war crime against the English language means, "I don't know."

Buyer-Seller Relationship

"It is not from the benevolence of the butcher, the brewer or the baker that we expect our dinner, but from their regard to their own interest."

—Adam Smith

The hot air of talk is as important to a salesman as a cool breeze is to the yachtsman: neither can make his landing without some wind. Some salesmen, however, have learned to minimize the use of small talk and have become outstanding listeners. They realize that many prospective purchasers can talk themselves into buying. Other salesmen continue to use overkill to get a sale and often blow it by talking too much. They do not realize that by relying only on clichés they rob their talk of essential relevance to the buyer's needs. A statement beginning "You will get more than you bargain for" [CONVINCER] unconsciously admits this. In this instance the salesman's meta-talk has put him beyond his listener. A "Dear Abby" column points up the fact that most of us have difficulty in listening to ourselves and probably don't listen to others as often as we should. An indignant lady wrote: "I had some guests over one evening, and while we were eating dinner the gentleman at my left asked, 'Do you mind if I smoke?' I smiled very politely, and replied, 'I'd rather you waited until after dinner.' He then took some cigarettes out of his pocket and proceeded to smoke!"

The culprit obviously interpreted a very polite smile for assent to his implied request to smoke and completely ignored the verbal message. He may also have assumed that no one could say "No" to any request he might make.

Unsuccessful salesmen, relying on clichés and charm, often deceive themselves in the same way.

Questions are vital of course to the buyer-seller relationship. However, people have become very sophisticated and a deal can be destroyed if questions are too frequently answered with questions: "How much will it cost me?" brings the reply, "How much do you think it should cost you?" This device to avoid saying "I don't know" can quickly degenerate into a downward spiral of increasingly hostile questions and evasive answers. An evasive technique may be effective in cross-examination, but remember that the lawyer and witness are not trying to "sell" each other. It is not necessary for a good salesman to have "all the answers." That too is cliché thinking. A salesman who admits he doesn't have the answer and proceeds to find it, in his eagerness to learn the truth and satisfy his customer, is creating a firm relationship.

When a buyer or seller says he will "try" to do something, he is often signaling that you should be prepared for his future inability to produce. If you are confronted with a promise to "try" [FOREBODER] to get certain terms on a deal, be ready to hear sometime later, "Well, I tried" (and failed). Frequent cost overruns on defense contracts would indicate that this and similar clichés ("I'll see what I can do," "We will make every effort") are used far too often in government contract dealings. On the individual level as well as the corporate, "trying" is the meta-talk of one preparing to be an underachiever. Salesmen who are successful prepare to fulfill their business commitments and get things done. They will very likely be treated as equals by the buyer in what then becomes a cooperative endeavor.

"Trying" puts a distance between the subject and the desired object because the infinitive "to do" is much weaker than the active use of the verb, "I will do it." Similarly the person who relates well to others in a buyer-seller situation will avoid other indications of distance. A financial column recently had a good example of a deal gone sour. A man had bought stock in a new electronics company but now was unable to get any information from the company. In an attempt to excuse his mistake he put as much distance as he possibly could between the stocks and himself: "I had no qualms about the investment because the president-and-founder was well known to me." When he first bought the stock he may very well have said, "Of course it's good. I know the founder" [CONVINCER].

Not all such distance-putting verbal devices are the result of injured pride. Many of us try to soften criticism by putting a string of words between "I" or "we" and the complaint: "I don't know how to say this . . ." [SOFTENER]; "I am doing this for your own good . . ."; "We've done business for a long time . . ."; "I wish I didn't have to say this but . . ." All of these clichés leave an impression that there is something not quite right about offering criticism. Yet it is often necessary to straighten out a relationship that has taken a wrong turn. Many successful executives are very aggressive and seldom waste time in softening criticism. So long as the criticism is valid and is kept impersonal this may be a good way for them to handle the problem. A frank revelation of a partner's feelings can actually improve a relationship by removing the "polite" distance between the two.

Criticism is usually the prerogative of the buyer, and in less than perfect buyer-seller relationships, so is praise. Some salesmen make the mistake of trying desperately to win approval by frantic meta-talk: "I'll tell you what I am going to do for you"; "I just happen to have . . ."; "Boy, do I have a deal for you" [INTERESTERS]. One would think that these clichés would have vanished with the snake-oil peddlers, but they still are the mainstays of many selling "techniques," particularly telephone solicitors. "Let the buyer beware" is the motto that flashes in the listener's mind in such situations.

Other salesmen attempt to prop up their sagging credibility by becoming defensive about imagined accusations: "What do you mean by that?"; "Do you want more proof?"; "The reason I did it was . . ."; "My intention in this was to . . ."; "It's just that . . ."; "Are you trying to tell me that . . ."; "Now wait a minute!" [DEFENDERS]. None of these phrases has ever revived a sagging relationship. They just push it further downhill.

SUPERIOR-SUBORDINATE RELATIONSHIP

"To be humble to superiors is duty, to equals courtesy, to inferiors nobleness."

—BENJAMIN FRANKLIN

Meta-talk abounds in relationships between superiors and subordinates, particularly those characterized by a lack of openness. An aware employee would recognize at once that if his boss says, "I want there to be complete frankness between us at all times" [SOFTENER], he may really be saying, "Don't tell me anything I don't want to hear." No superior can obtain frankness or any other quality from an employee merely by requesting it. He may get a semblance of frankness or honesty in this way. To achieve an open relationship, however, trust must first be established. Similarly, statements such as "This is the way I'd like to see it done" [DOWNER] can really mean, "You are incapable of thinking for yourself. *I'm the only one who thinks around here.*" The boss who signals this through his meta-talk is not getting as much as he should from his employee. No intelligent person enjoys a relationship that limits his creative ability to come up with alternatives to problems, and "This is the *only* way" certainly does that.

If employees confident of their abilities resent such signals from their superiors, less confident subordinates employ meta-talk to beg for reassurance while denying any weakness in their performance. "On the whole . . ." and "Under the circumstances . . ." often introduce these self-serving statements: "On the whole I'm satisfied with the job I did"; "Under the circumstances, I don't see how I could have done anything differently" [DEFENDERS]. The meta-talk of these statements is, "I don't have any specific strong points to bring out, so I'll generalize."

An employer may say, "On the whole, your idea sounds all right" [DOWNER]. If he follows up with, "Let me sleep on it," chances are he doesn't think it is important enough to keep him awake. The employee who eagerly awaits the next day to get the verdict is in for a jolting disappointment.

Quite naturally, money and its allocation produces a great deal of meta-talk in superior-subordinate relationships. Oddly, some employees can be quite forthright and aggressive about getting every penny of a proposed departmental budget, let us say, and yet be very reluctant to discuss their personal financial needs for fear of being rebuffed. Asking for raises and forestalling such requests provide cartoonists with limitless material. They also can be time-consuming in offices where there is no open communication between employee and boss. One seemingly open conversation from the superior might go like this: "Dave, this company is confronted by a strong competitive market dominated by buyers. In order to survive, we must minimize all costs in order to compete" [FOREBODER]. The subordinate has no difficulty translating this. It means, "Don't expect any increase in pay" or "You're not going to get the increase I promised you last year." For some timid souls the meta-talk is enough, but a more desperate one might venture: "I was wondering how you felt about considering giving me a raise?" [FOREBODER]. Note the distance put between "I" and "raise." It almost becomes an abstract speculation. Therefore, if it is answered with a terse "lousy!" the employee can gracefully but quickly take cover.

A stronger person might preface his request with what he hopes are rhetorical questions: "Do you like my performance?" or, "Have you found any significant weaknesses in my department?" [CONTINUERS]. If the answers are favorable, he can then proceed with, "In view of that fact . . ." or, "Considering that . . ." Both are meta-talk for "I am too good to refuse." The superior may simply acknowledge that fact or say, "I'll tell you what . . ." [FOREBODER] meaning, "You're not going to get a pay increase that easily." A negotiating situation at least has been set up.

As with all relationships, those between superiors and subordinates run the gamut from destructive to highly satisfying to both parties. Dickens' *Oliver Twist* presents a scene that with a few changes might be appropriate for some offices today:

Oliver in the workhouse has been driven by hunger to ask for a supplement to his meager rations:

> "Please, sir, I want some more."
> There was a general start. Horror was depicted on every countenance.

"For more!" said Mr. Lambkins. "Compose yourself,
Bumble, and answer me distinctly. Do I understand
that he asked for more, after he had eaten the supper
allotted by the dietary?"

"He did, sir," replied Bumble.

"That boy will be hung," said the gentleman in the
white waistcoat. "I know that boy will be hung."

At the other extreme is a positive, supportive, superior-
subordinate relationship. Here there is a minimum of meta-
talk. The superior has indicated by his actions and words
that he has confidence in his subordinate's ability to do his
job well and creatively. The employee has no need to seek
reassurance through meta-talk or unrealistic rewards. He
knows where he stands. Everyone does.

Lovers' Relationship

"Women have simple tastes. They can get pleasure out
of conversation of children in arms and men in love."
                                        –H. L. Mencken

The relationship between lovers is not characterized by stability and longevity. Most couples actively seek a
conclusion, the state of matrimony, a different relationship.
This is borne out by the fact that, in the world's literature,
few great lovers are married. The lovers' span of time is
relatively brief. This period is packed with heightened emotions which reach a peak that will probably never be reached
again in other relationships. Courtship and the curious behavior of people involved in love have provided writers
through the centuries with a rich lode of comic and tragic

plots. Courtship is a preliminary fact-finding session for marriage, the continuing marathon negotiation. People in love look at each other; in marriage, hopefully, they look in the same direction. To a person in love the most trivial fact ("You like chocolate ice cream! Why, I like chocolate ice cream too!") is transformed into an earth-shaking revelation. The reason is simple: both parties are gathering facts to determine whether or not they are compatible. At the time this seems the most important task in the world. During this period also there is a great deal of soul-searching over whether one is "worthy" of the other. "Would you like me better if I . . ." [SOFTENER] is a typical bit of meta-talk, asking for approval.

After the fact-finding phase is over—and the facts are found to be satisfactory—emotions become somewhat less tempestuous and attitudes more objective. The masking of love is as difficult as faking it. This is the time when doubts are aired: "Are you getting anything out of this?" [FORE-BODER] indicates that neither one is; "Of course I love you but give me a little more time" [FOREBODER] can mean "I want to shop around some more"; "Will you always love me?" expresses doubt that their relationship is a lifelong commitment; "Do you think we are doing the right thing?" means "We aren't doing the right thing."

Evasions also creep into the meta-talk. "You want to know why I did it?" [DEFENDER] gives the partner a little time to think up a good reason, especially if followed with, "I'll tell you why I did it." Similarly, these are designed to gain time: "Before you say anything I want to . . ."; "Now, it isn't as bad as it looks"; or "Just give me a chance to explain the whole thing" [DEFENDERS]. "I should have known you wouldn't trust me" transfers the blame for the situation to the suspicious partner, gains time and diverts the conversation at least for a moment from the troublesome subject.

In a hypothetical situation of a male caught in a compromising situation, the following meta-talk might take place:

"Ralph, who was that girl you were kissing?" ("Try to get out of this!")

"Who do you mean?" ("Let me think.")

"You know perfectly well who I mean. That girl." ("You're going to lie to me.")

"Oh, her! I'm glad you asked me." ("Now, let's see. What can I say?")

"Well, I'm waiting." ("I am a stern but fair judge.")

"Stella, honey, you're not going to believe this but . . ." (He doesn't believe it either.)

"Tell me anyway." ("If you come clean, I might forgive you.")

"Didn't I ever tell you about her, Stella?" ("No, I didn't, and now I have to think of a good reason why I didn't.")

"No, you didn't." (Here the girl loses control of the conversation. The subject has become the other girl and the kiss is no longer even a part of it.)

"Oh, I know . . ." ("Let's try this one on for size.")

"But why were you kissing her?" ("I'm not easily diverted.")

"Oh, that! If-uh-she hadn't told me she had just got engaged, I never would have dreamed of kissing her." ("Let's get as far away from this as possible.")

"Oh!" ("I don't believe it but I can't prove it isn't true, so I'll accept it.")

Lovers use negative statements quite often to state a desire and to ask the other partner to "convince" them that this is the right thing to do: "I really can't stay" [CON-TINUER] means "I want to stay all night"; "I can't go there looking like this, can I?" means "Please don't make me clean up"; "I'll never speak to you again!" means "Make me talk." Admittedly, these and similar devices are immature ways of communicating desires, but in a successful relationship the talk will open up and the partners will not have to rely on pretended weaknesses to get their way.

Many women continue to feign weakness and passivity in their adult lives, seeming to acquiesce always to men's desires. This is reflected in the *True Confession* type of magazine and in hoary old jokes men like to tell: If a lady says "no" she means "maybe"; if she says "maybe" she means "yes"; if she says "yes" she's really no lady. For whatever consolation it may be, we can only repeat an old wish: Love and the measles—may we all go through the experiences early in life.

viii
SITUATIONS

"So in every individual the two trends, one towards personal happiness and the other towards unity with the rest of humanity, must contend with each other."

—SIGMUND FREUD

In supportive relationships we deal with known qualities in ourselves and in our partners. To a degree we can anticipate the probable response of our partner and do not need to search blindly for what his words mean. In many life situations this certainty does not exist. Not only the person but the meanings he attaches to words are unknown. As a result we must grope to reach an understanding of the person involved with us in a situation. It is a difficult but not impossible task if we are fully aware of the hidden meanings that gestures and meta-talk can convey.

Why bother? Because, as John Donne observed, "No man is an island, entire of itself"; we cannot escape situations. We must in some way deal with them, even if we only refuse to become involved. More important, situations are the raw material for establishing relationships. Successful people know the value of sizing up every situation to see if it is capable of initiating a mutually beneficial relationship. Others react by making a cliché of every situation. "Small world, isn't it, meeting a fellow American in Paris? Do you know Smith, Jones and Thomas in Chicago?" epitomizes this type of response, and the speaker makes the world very small indeed. Others put an insurmountable distance between themselves and the other parties in a situation. "Pleased to have met you" has buried many a potential friendship.

There are some people who milk any situation for all it is worth. An examination of the meta-talk is revealing. The famous hassle over whether or not Bobby Fischer would play in the world's chess championship match in Iceland is a case in point. It showed a once-in-a-lifetime situation and how Fischer handled it. He demanded a cut of the gate receipts in addition to the prize money. When the match promoters turned this down, he refused to leave for Iceland. At last the impasse was broken when a London banker put up $130,000 in additional prize money. Fischer commented, "I gotta accept it. It's a stupendous offer, incredible and generous and brave" [CONTINUER]. In ordinary English, "I gotta" means "I have an obligation," but an obligation to whom or what? Fischer's lawyer attempted to provide an answer: "It was the principle. He felt Iceland wasn't treating this match or his countrymen with the dignity that it and they deserved." The meta-talk in both statements seems to be that money equals dignity, a rather dubious "principle" to base an argument on. We have not been able to figure out, however, why the banker was "brave" in making the offer. If, however, gaining the news headlines of the world for chess was the motive, it certainly was successful.

Most of us do not deal with our daily situations constructively. We avoid the challenge of finding new ways to deal with people. Each day consists of stock scenes in which we encourage others to play the same role over and over again. Our reactions, as from an audience, may range from "Here's Charlie. He's always good for a laugh" to "There's Ed. He's always trying to impress you." Both our observations are perhaps justified by Charlie and Eddie's stereotyped roles. If, however, you are participating, ask yourself if you have ever tried to get more than a laugh out of Charlie or a boast from Ed. Of course it may be difficult, but an effort should be made.

There are those who seemingly do not at first fall into the cliché pattern. They never have an opinion of their own (or at least they never would venture to reveal it). They are the passive receptacles of other people's opinions, which they take great pains to discover, then feed back to the object of their attention. They usually introduce their borrowed opinions with such phrases as "Don't you think that . . . ," "Isn't it true . . . ," or "Shouldn't we look at it this way?" [SOFTENERS]. It is very satisfying to the ego to be agreed with in this quite subtle way. But if you find your companion shares your taste for fried grasshoppers and Krafft-Ebing you may discover that you have not begun a wonderful new relationship but that you have been had. People with massive egos are usually the victims of this tactic. After all, do you expect anyone to agree with you one hundred percent of the time?

The trouble with yes-men is that they offer no room for a relationship to grow. One plus zero equals one, but when the ideas and aspirations of two people are combined, the cumulative result of each person's thinking is at least doubled. Let's examine some of the situations in business and in personal life that grow or are aborted by meta-talk.

Business Situations

"Even the wisest among men welcome people who bring
money more than those who take it away."
—G. C. Lichtenberg

Since many people view business as a highly competitive win/lose situation, it is not surprising that meta-talk in the business world often deals with evaluations and defensive excuses for failure. A boss asking an employee, "What do you think that I should do?" [HIDING THE HALO] seems to be asking for an evaluation. However, he is offering an evaluation: "I can't handle it but I don't think you can either." Or he may say, "That was a very thorough presentation and I want you to know I appreciate that you did it on your own time." He means, "You're lucky it wasn't on my time. Now get back to distributing the mail."

Similar statements are what we call "sandwich" statements. You start with a slice of praise, add a filling of criticism and top it off with some other negative observation. An example is, "You did a good job on that (compliment) but you didn't complete the final invoicing correctly (criticism). Think you'll get the next one right? (doubt)." Sandwich statements are so common that many listeners do not even hear the compliment. They wait for the inevitable "but" and in the meantime their minds scramble wildly to find an excuse. This in turn is interrupted by the unanswerable question at the end. Of course, there has been no effective communication; therefore, neither party benefits from the exchange and the employee can only feel resentment.

Some employees avoid a sandwich statement by saying

only what they know will please the boss: his own words and thoughts. These they carefully memorize, no matter how misguided or wrong-headed they may be, and serve them up at suitable intervals. Often they preface their remarks with, "Tell me if I'm wrong." This is a perfectly safe thing to say since any boss that can be taken in by this ruse is also probably not going to be critical of his own ideas. Like the sandwich statement, this situation is destructive. Words are used as weapons, not as instruments for transmitting and sharing ideas.

There are certain "buzz" words that have become clichés. These are used to obtain feedback and may have a limited positive use. However, when used to excess, such expressions as "Right?" "Is that clear?" "Okay?" "Check?" "Do you follow?" are verbal tics that unconsciously express a doubt that the listener is capable of clearly understanding anything. They also become unreliable guides since they practically demand an affirmative answer. The speaker assumes he will get one and rushes on, ignoring verbal and nonverbal feedback. These clichés also limit the scope of any conversation. There is a hidden assumption that for every problem there is but one correct and one incorrect solution. Most of life's problems do not lend themselves to such a simplistic approach. No successful businessman can afford to come up with "the" solution. Generally, there are many alternatives, one of which seems especially appropriate in a given time and place. It often takes time and a supportive relationship to come up with an appropriate answer. Clichés only hamper the process.

Some executives attempt to conceal their sense of self-importance with statements that attempt to minimize their ability or power: "In my humble opinion . . ."; "May I make a modest suggestion?"; "If I may venture an idea

. . . "; "Far be it from me to disagree . . ." [HIDING THE HALO]. Probably no one is fooled by such preliminary statements, but subordinates are alerted that a "great thought of Western man" is about to make its appearance and they had better like it. It is unwise to use this tactic on a superior, however. When Lyndon Johnson was President he met with railroad executives in an attempt to settle a strike. He had union agreement on a proposed settlement, but Johnson felt that management was opposed to it. Albin Krebs describes the scene:

> When one management representative began the meeting with "I'm just an old country boy . . .," old country boy Lyndon Johnson imperiously shushed him. "Hold it," he snapped, "stop right there. When I hear that around this town, I put my hand on my billfold. Don't start that with me."
>
> The astonished butt of the Presidential dressing-down joined the laughter and said, "By God, I was just going to say that I'm ready to sign up." Mr. Johnson said later that he believed "that broke the deadlock, but of course I'll never know what he was going to say when I broke in."

Far be it from us to second-guess a President [SOFTENER], but "I was *just* going to say . . ." was probably meta-talk for "I was not going to say that at all." A similar device is to say, "I don't want to seem . . ." [SOFTENER]. The speaker denies he is suspicious, doubtful, angry, upset, or whatever, but is he? Yes, of course.

When children use the statement, "Wait a minute," it literally means that you are going too fast for them and they need time to catch up. When adults say it they may want to interrupt what you are saying with a thought of their own or they may be objecting to what you have just said. The latter meta-talk can provide you with the valuable clue that you are not communicating effectively. Take, for example, a seasoned executive who has just been reorganized out of a job. A well-intentioned friend, determined to "help" him, begins to offer "off the top of his head" [HIDING THE HALO] (meaning, "I'm a genius, I can turn out ideas like popcorn") solutions to his employment problem. Suddenly, the executive interrupts with "Now wait a minute!" [DEFENDER]. What does the meta-talk mean? The friend has made the hidden assumption that the executive is over the hill and incapable of making a decision for himself. He must be "told" what to do. The "Wait a minute" is a protest from the victim who is being talked *to*, not communicated *with*. The conversation has added to his problems and increased his self-doubts. In a supportive relationship, this would not happen. The priorities would be reversed: instead of the friend offering solutions to assumed problems, the problems would be thoroughly analyzed and, more important, the executive's aims and aspirations for the future would shape proposed solutions to the problems. The term "Job's comforters" means those who discourage or depress while seeming to give consolation. These abound in both business and social situations. Don't be one. Communicate!

SOCIAL SITUATIONS

"She sits tormenting every guest,
Nor gives her tongue one moment's rest,
In phrases batter'd stale and trite,
Which modern ladies call polite."
—JONATHAN SWIFT

In many cities in the United States you are required to have the exact fare for buses. Taxi drivers in New York City are not required to give change for more than five dollars. Just as it is necessary to have small change to travel in the cities, to travel in most social circles it is necessary to have small talk. This is the usual initial fare that must be paid to start an ordinary conversation. Small talk consists of a number of conventional phrases, statements, and questions. Although similar to clichés, they serve an important purpose as starters in a ritual dance that determines whether two people can break out of an egocentric form and become friends. The breakthrough may come at any time. "How are you?" [SOFTENER] usually elicits a "Fine, thank you," if it is answered at all. So expected is this that many people would then say, "That's wonderful!" even if the reply had been, "I'm at death's door." But think of the potential for friendship if both the questioner and the listener were hypochondriacs and the response was "Terrible" followed by a long explanation of why.

Conventional talk is an attempt to discover common ground with a stranger. Most people feel uncomfortable when questioned by a person they do not know well unless the questions are the expected traditional ones, or they are informed as to what is being attempted. They fear that they may be giving away something that could endanger them, and they are reluctant to do that except with friends. As a result, the less fear-producing questions are often indirect ("Are you a writer?" [SOFTENER] instead of "What do you do?") or only hinted at ("I think the President is doing a splendid job" instead of "What are your politics?"). Note that in both cases information is traded for information: "If you are a writer, I could become very much interested in you"; "If you believe as I do, we would have a common bond." In this way we build on a social situation, trading bits of information about ourselves, seeing if we can establish a relationship.

The use of immediacy and distance often illuminates how well the process is going:

"You may disagree, but I like modern art."
"I know too little about it to form an opinion, but if someone would teach me, perhaps I'd like it."
"We could learn about it together."
"When do we start?"

The process may also go badly:

"I felt the bombing was unfortunate but necessary."
"How can you say that? It was plain murder."
"That's what those men in Hanoi want us to believe."
"See you around sometime."

The first example shows an open attitude on both sides. They are ready to embark on a cooperative effort. In the second example, attitudes are hard and unyielding. Both are saying, "You either agree with me or you are the enemy." This provides a very poor climate for the relationship to grow.

Some people, either through unconscious malice or from ignorance of what their words mean, derail every attempt at communication. Their standard cliché is, "Did I say something wrong?" [DEFENDER] which is not a question but an admission that they have. These essentially lonely people perversely sidetrack all attempts to exchange emotions and thoughts and then complain they have "no one to talk to" —not "talk with" but "talk to," or, more accurately, "talk at." They can do this by adopting an either/or attitude:

"You *must* try my pumpkin cake."
"Oh, I like applesauce cake so much better."

Thus a relationship potential is destroyed because only one kind of cake can be good. Other destructive people use "irrelevant" questions to get across a hostile message. One lady asked an advice column if her husband had a complex because he "barks at me and jumps down my throat all the time when I ask him a question. He says I mean something by everything I ask. Recently his nephew was married and I asked him if the nephew had found a job yet." The husband may or may not have a "complex" but he certainly has an awareness of meta-talk.

For some, meta-talk in social situations consists of three words: "Unhum," "Hunuh," and "Maybe." These people have an inflated opinion not only of their social appeal but of their penetrating psychological insights. They get a false sense of power because their three words and a poker face can reduce an insecure person to a babbling idiot. Policemen have relied on this device since crime (or the police department) began. The unsure victim will talk compulsively, saying anything to break the dreadful silence, and it is astonishing how most urban Americans, at least, hate silence. They will churn out words, admit anything, say anything, to avoid lulls in conversations. Our advice is, if so involved, try to change it or to get out fast. This is not a relationship—it is worse than a third degree.

There are compulsive talkers who are driven not by insecurity but by vanity. Their meta-talk does not necessarily deal with clichés, it is merely one-dimensional: concerned with "I." They are easily recognized by all who appreciate plain talk. Lady Astor once told a temperance meeting: "I would rather commit adultery than drink a glass of beer." A hoarse male voice in the audience responded, "Who wouldn't?" This had the makings of the start of a beautiful relationship if both the man and the woman could have agreed on what these words "really" meant. Too many of us waste too much energy in searching for the narrowly interpreted specifics that separate us rather than for broad areas of agreement that can bring us together.

SITUATIONS WITH ACQUAINTANCES AND FRIENDS

"A man of active and resilient mind outwears his friendships just as certainly as he outwears his love affairs, his politics, and his epistemology."

—H. L. MENCKEN

Let us consider a young man on his first date with an interesting young woman. He becomes curious when during the course of the evening she mentions "a friend of mine." Is that friend a man or a woman? Now reverse the situation. The young man mentions "a friend of mine." Now she wonders whether the friend to whom he is referring is a man or a woman.

Curiously, whether the man or the woman makes the reference, the answer is the same—a man. Both would, of course, also use "girlfriend" to designate the opposite sex. A woman's "friend" and a man's "girlfriend" indicate at least some degree of involvement which the new acquaintance, if interested, will surely want more information about.

There is also a variation of this rule—when a "friend of mine" means "I." This is a method used for seeking personal advice without acknowledgment that the problem is personal also. It is utilized to put a distance between the giver and receiver of the advice. Thus the person who says, "A friend of mine has a problem," is trying to conceal his involvement or attempting to get "free" advice which he then can either accept or reject without any sense of gratitude. If the giver of the advice does not see through this play-acting, the advice will probably be as amateurish as he is.

Many people seek to get something out of a situation without being prepared to add anything of themselves. Occasionally they may obtain a temporary advantage over some unsuspecting soul, but the results rarely bring a permanent benefit. Such people are like the Consolidated Edison computer that dunned a young New Yorker for an unpaid bill. It threatened to cut off service unless she paid what she owed—$0.00. Finally, the girl sent in a check for $0.00 and the notices stopped. The computer had received its due. Payment in this amount is the usual lot of those who try to use friends and acquaintances only for their own advantage.

A common impediment to establishing a friendly relationship is to set up a friend or acquaintance as the judge of actions or words that should be ruled on by one's own conscience or experience. In this way one can prepare to escape responsibility for one's actions by blaming them on another. Some examples: "Do you think I talk too much?" [DEFENDER] ("I do but would be embarrassed to admit it"); "Would you rather I leave now?" ("I've stayed too long but I don't know how to go"); "Are you interested in hearing about Mary?" ("I want to gossip but only if you will take the responsibility"); "You don't think I went too far, do you?" [DEFENDER] ("Yes, I did, but tell me I didn't"). Acquaintances and casual friends are made to feel awkward by such questions. A frank answer is virtually ruled out because it might be "rude." Yet no one likes to be coerced into giving an answer and taking the blame for the consequences.

A less harmful type of meta-talk does not necessarily affect a budding relationship but it portrays the speaker as weak and indecisive. It depends on the use of the subjunctive mood to indicate the distance between the statement and reality: "I really should call Mary" [DELAYER], instead of "I'll call Mary right now"; "I really should go on a diet" ("But I won't"); "I really should go over there and take a look for myself" ("I don't want to face reality"). People who make such statements have a vague feeling of guilt but are unwilling to use self-discipline to resolve the problem. They are weak candidates for an enduring relationship unless the other party likes to bolster his own ego by taking command. But that does not make for a balanced relationship either. When he does take command and bungles the job, his defense is likely to be, "I was only trying to help" [DEFENDER]. Here again "only" is used to minimize involvement. An alternative is to ask, "Did I do anything wrong?" That in turn brings the reply, "No, but . . ." which means "Yes."

Domineering people are also very fond of statements that begin, "I don't want to . . ." [SOFTENER] followed by a "but" [DOWNER]. This is somewhat more explicit meta-talk than "Yes, but . . ." and "No, but . . ."; however, it serves the same purpose. You deny what you are about to say as a way of affirming it: "I don't like to sound like an old fogy, but I don't like long hair on boys" ("Cut it off at once!"); "I don't like to seem nosy, but what were you doing out at two in the morning?" ("Come clean!"); "I don't like to sound like I'm bragging, but I won" [HIDING THE HALO] ("I'm wonderful. Admire me"); "I don't want to sound like I'm telling you what to do, but I'd . . ." [PLEADER] ("Do it my way!"); "I don't like to press you, but I could use the money you owe me" [PLEADER] ("Pay up or else").

For your consideration we offer Frank Crane's definition of friendship: "What is a friend? I will tell you. It is a person with whom you dare to be yourself."

SITUATIONS WITH STRANGERS

"Conversations between Adam and Eve must have been difficult at times because they had nobody to talk about."
—AGNES REPPLIER

Dr. Karl Menninger in *Love Against Hate* offers a translation of "Got a flat?" in terms of its psychological meaning: "Hello—I see you are in trouble. I am a stranger to you but I might be your friend now that I have a chance to be if I had any assurance that my friendship would be welcomed. Are you approachable? Are you a decent fellow? Would you appreciate it if I helped you? I would like to do so but I don't want to be rebuffed. This is what my voice sounds like. What does your voice sound like?"

These and similar statements and questions are likely to be implicit in any introductory remark by a stranger. The opening words indicate that he at least wants to change the situation from casual proximity to something more meaningful, otherwise he would be silent or utter a terse greeting and turn away. However, how effective is the meta-talk of "Got a flat?" Not very. The other person is upset by the situation he is in and is concentrating wholly on his problem. The last thing he wants to do is answer questions, especially stupid questions about the obvious. A statement about the condition would be better: "I see you have a flat." This indicates a certain sharing of the problem and implies an offer to help. The other person can then make his choice: "Yes, and it's miles to the nearest service station" (acceptance) or "I can take care of it" (rejection). At the very least, the other person has been drawn into communicating something about the type of person he is and how he reacts to the stranger.

Plain clichés are ineffective in "breaking the ice" with a stranger. "Nice day, isn't it?" can be answered with "yes," "no," or a grunt—all virtually reflex actions. No communication has taken place except for one vital thing. If the other person is alert to meta-talk, he knows that the stranger likes to talk and probably will not listen; there will not be an exchange of views but rather a rehash of stale experiences and impressions in a droning monologue. As the clichés begin to roll from a stranger's lips, you will probably determine to keep the situation as one between strangers.

Sholem Aleichem tells a delightful story of an old man on a train confronted with a cliché:

> The young man standing next to him asked, "What time is it?" The old man refused to reply. The young man moved on. The old man's friend, sensing something was wrong, asked, "Why were you so discourteous to the young man asking for the time?" The old man answered, "If I had given him the time of day, next he would want to know where I'm going. Then we might talk about our interests. If we did that, he might invite himself to my house for dinner. If he did, he would meet my lovely daughter. If he met her, they would both fall in love. I don't want my daughter marrying someone who can't afford a watch."

Many people in reacting to strangers reason in much the same way as the old man on the train, assumption following assumption with breathtaking speed until the conclusion is reached almost instantaneously: "I don't want to talk to this person." The reason for rejection may range from the wildly improbable ("He looks like a rapist to me") to the plausible ("He wants to know too much"). Often unskilled use of questions triggers the latter reaction. Questions which ask for information without indicating the reason for wanting the information can turn what should be an attempt at communication into a cross-examination. People tend to be anxious about questions that ask for specific facts if they do not know how this will commit them. They are much more open if the questions on the stranger's part merely seek their opinions or beliefs.

In some languages the word for enemy and stranger is the same. In those cultures making friends is not easy. In English, the word "stranger" originally meant "foreigner" and implies a great distance between two people. Narrowing that gap should be a conscious concern of anyone who wants to get the most out of life. Meeting a stranger should be done with an open mind, however, not with the question "What's in it for me?" Joseph P. Lash, in the biography *Eleanor and Franklin*, tells of the family's reactions to Mrs. Roosevelt's suggestion that they have a Christmas party for the children of the Women's Trade Union League members. Sara Roosevelt was horrified—"The diseases the two boys might pick up." Franklin, Jr., and John, however, approved of the idea. Invitations were sent out in their names and Eleanor purchased the gifts. "At the last moment, her boys balked; they could not understand 'giving presents': Christmas was a time for 'getting' presents." Too often fear and distrust of strangers or a calculated approach destroys any chance of changing the status of a stranger to one of associate in a meaningful relationship.

Unhappy Situations

"New happiness too we must learn to bear."
—Marie von Ebner-Eschenbach

Unhappy situations in our daily affairs tend to make us somewhat timid. In such cases we attempt to put as much distance as we can between ourselves and the unpleasant fact of life. Notice how quickly we change from present to past tense when a person dies. There is a complete change of gears in most of us. We go from a critical attitude ("He's nothing but a freeloader") to uncritical praise ("He was always so good-natured!"). This is a great distance to travel in such a brief time and quickly relegates the subject to the past. "He will long be remembered" achieves the same result by use of the passive voice. Long be remembered by whom? Almost certainly not by the speaker. In contrast, Edwin Stanton's remark on the death of Lincoln, "Now he belongs to the ages," places the subject in perspective, yet the use of the present tense suggests a continuing influence in spite of death.

Funerals are usually rare occurrences for most of us and we find ourselves acting uncomfortable when we attend them. To ease this feeling clichés abound as emotions are concealed or displaced: "Words cannot express what I felt about him" [PLEADER] ("I would prefer not to express my feelings" or " I have no feeling"); "I can't tell you how I felt when I heard" [CONVINCER]. ("Well, actually, I wasn't aware of my feelings"); "What can you say at a time like this?" ("I would prefer not finding out"); "If there's ever anything I can do for you, please let me know" [DELAYER] ("By putting it off I hope I won't be called on"); "We all will miss him" ("I prefer to be part of an anonymous group"); "Why did it have to happen to him?" ("Just so it doesn't include me"); "Who could have dreamed it would end this way?" ("I have—many times"); "She died so young" ("I now feel very insecure").

Displacement plays a large role in many funerals. This meta-talk does not usually take the form of clichés, the reason being that the words, however improbable, must fit the individual situation. Displacement is easy to recognize. When it takes place, someone (anyone but the dear departed and the speaker) is to "blame." Doctors, relatives, friends and enemies are blamed for the present condition of the deceased. "If only . . ." [JUDGER] is a popular introduction to these accusations: "If only he had gone to the doctor I suggested"; "If only he had acted like a husband should, she would be alive today"; "If only her mother had made her go to a doctor"; "If only he hadn't been so stupid!"; "If only he hadn't hated her so much!" The "only" gives the meta-talk meaning. The "only" reason for the death is "them." The speaker is thus able to displace any feeling of guilt over not having liked the dead person as well as he might have, or he simply feels guilt over still being alive.

In the business world a firing is comparable to a funeral, only the boss must supply the corpse. Some go about their work "in a businesslike manner," ready—even eager—to get it over with. This was true in a story related by a young girl working her way through college and employed in the commissary of a large restaurant chain. She sliced pies. Her job was to fit a form over the pie, slip a knife through the slots, and slice the pie into uniform pieces. Late each day the company president toured the commissary. Quitting time was five o'clock and exactly at five o'clock she stopped working. She left the pastry bench with a knife still sticking out of a half-cut pie. She was stopped by the president who said sadly but firmly, "Miss, I don't think you're interested in your job. You're fired!" Rarely today would we hear such a surprisingly straightforward statement. Unions and other watchdogs are looking over management's shoulder. Forthright statements are out; they would be repeated at union arbitration hearings. Meta-talk has taken their place. It is no longer proper to say, "Throw the rascal out!" but rather, "Due to the extensive reorganization we have recently undertaken, we have found that the office of assistant for paper clips no longer fits into our organization chart. Therefore after much agonizing over the problem, we have decided to abolish the position. Mr. John Smith, who has held this position, has decided to seek employment elsewhere so that he can use his great knowledge of this field to its maximum advantage." It still means "Throw the rascal out!" but you can't quite put your finger on where it says that.

Some executives begin such statements with "I wish I didn't have to . . ." [FOREBODER]. There are several levels of meta-talk involved here. On the superficial level it means, "I'm exaggerating. I don't 'hate' to do anything that involves my financial well-being. However, you are going to hate what I am about to say since it threatens your financial status."

We have found than an introductory clause more probably has meta-talk meaning. In many negotiating sessions the words mean, "This is my offer. There can be and will be no alternatives to it. Accept it as is or else." If challenged with, "You're not interested in any other way!" the response is likely to be, "What are you talking about?" ("I know exactly what you mean but I don't like your attitude"). In this way we shut off a mutual search for creative alternatives and condemn ourselves to a life of either/or choices. There is probably no sadder state of existence than this voluntary imprisonment of the mind.

POLITICIANS AND META-TALK

"But what good came of it at last?"
  Quoth Little Peterkin.
"Why that I cannot tell," said he,
"But 'twas a famous victory."
        —ROBERT SOUTHEY, "The Battle of Blenheim"

Today, Friedrich Nietzsche's observation seems to have become even more valid than when it was first made. He said, "A politician divides mankind into two classes:

tools and enemies. That means that he knows only one class: enemies." With true American efficiency, politicians and other spokesmen for the United States Government seem to have arrived at Orwell's 1984 well ahead of time. War is peace, a cease-fire is peace with honor, our traditional enemies are our friends, and our traditional allies our enemies, bombing targets are only what a "Pentagon spokesman" says they are regardless of what was hit, and those who cry that the emperor has no clothes on are liars. It is difficult in such situations to avoid the cynical conclusions that most public men lie and that when a politician says one thing he really means the exact opposite. Indeed, public opinion polls show that a majority of the American people do not believe business leaders any more than they do politicians.

In the emotionally fired-up atmosphere of charges and countercharges, it's "us" against "them." This makes for an exciting football game but is a terrible way to run a country. Lyndon Johnson liked to quote from the Bible, "Come let us reason together," which worked quite well in reconciling honest differences of opinion but not nearly as well in forcing people to accept a win/lose game plan. Since the Vietnam War dominated so much American time and energy during the last decade, it was natural that the Pentagon should emerge as spokesman, directly or indirectly, for the President and a majority of the Congress. If the country learned anything, it learned that military men could distort the English language with more skill than any vote-hungry politician. "The light at the end of the tunnel" became a grisly joke as the war dragged on. "Protective reaction strike" meant "We assume the enemy will try to shoot us down if we fly near enough, so let's fly over and bomb them first." But we did not learn the facts until long after the event, and, at the time, to consider military statements meta-talk would have been thought subversive.

Once in a while, however, the meta-talk came through loud and clear. Take the example of a young Navy pilot who flatly contradicted a charge by a fellow pilot that his squadron had participated under the guise of "protective reaction" in unauthorized raids on North Vietnam. In testimony before the Senate Armed Services Committee he was asked if he had met with senior officers before his appearance. He mentioned two immediate superiors, then "recalled" that he had also talked with the Chairman of the Joint Chiefs of Staff, the Chief of Naval Operations, and about twenty senior Navy officers. However, he assured the senators and newsmen later, he had only been urged "to tell the truth." Although he attempted to make it sound like a Cub Scout meeting, his use of "only" and the attempt to minimize twenty officers by at first mentioning only two indicate there was a great deal more to it than that.

Statesmen have long been regarded as much more competent at concealing facts than most of us. But as with the navy pilot, Dr. Henry Kissinger was tripped up by his meta-talk. He was talking about the 1972 war between India and Pakistan over Bangladesh. He told newsmen: "There have been some comments that the Administration is anti-Indian. This is totally inaccurate. India is a great country." Analysis of the meta-talk brings out these points: (1) "Some comments" tries to downgrade a strong belief by important people that the statement is true. Why else would a busy man like Dr. Kissinger waste his time on them?; (2) "totally" indicates that he protests too much; and (3) what does India's being "a great country" (great in what way?) have to do with the Administration's attitude? Fortunately, the country did not have to wait long for a thoroughgoing translation of this rather confusing comment. Within the week a "leak" of details of secret National Security Council sessions which took place prior to that very news conference, had Kissinger saying: "I am getting hell every half hour from the President that we are not being tough enough on India. He just called me again . . . he wants to tilt in favor of Pakistan."

Excuses for getting rid of critics reach a high art in Washington politics. Take the case of a former Air Force Deputy Assistant Secretary, for example. He made the mistake of revealing to Congress that the government had paid more than one billion in cost overruns on Lockheed's C-52 military transport plane. For this he was rewarded by a grateful government which first sent him to inspect a bowling alley in Thailand and then dismissed him. The Air Force Secretary explained why he had reached this difficult decision: "We have not found a suitable new position in which he could make a contribution." Perhaps the meta-talk could be translated: We don't like any of his contributions.

Bureaucratic meta-talk has been with us for a long time. The object seems to be to create an impenetrable thicket of words that no one can find fault with because no one can understand them. An example of this was an order issued by the Public Administration Bureau during World War II: "Such preparations shall be made as will completely obscure all Federal Buildings and nonfederal buildings occupied by the Federal Government during an air-raid for any period of time from visibility by reason of internal or external illumination." President Franklin D. Roosevelt saw beyond this bureaucratic obscurantism and directed, "Tell them that in a building where they have to keep work going, to put something across the windows."

Implied threats play a large role in some politicians' meta-talk. One example occurred when North Vietnam freed three American prisoners in the fall of 1972. They were placed in the charge of an antiwar group and flew home by a roundabout route to avoid military authorities who wanted to take them into custody before they reached the United States. This would have violated a condition under which the North Vietnamese had released them. Defense Secretary Melvin R. Laird, expressed the "hope" that the POW's would not be court-martialed. "Should charges be made, they will be looked at. I would hope no such charges would be made by any individual. However," he said, "if charges are filed, justice will be done and justice, as far as I'm concerned, as long as I'm here, will be tempered with a great, great deal of mercy." It is hard to escape the conclusion that Laird was saying, "Even if they've been playing footsie with those peaceniks, and I think they have, we won't ask for the extreme penalty."

President Nixon, long before the 1972 election, issued an overt threat that if his opponents tried to use the Vietnam War as an issue in the election campaign, he would "pull the rug out from under them." They did and he did. Dr. Kissinger announced days before the election that "Peace is at hand."

If you are confused by the apparent inability of politicians to tell the truth, view their statements with Lewis Carroll in mind:

> "But 'glory' doesn't mean 'a nice knockdown argument,' " Alice objected.
>
> "When *I* use a word," Humpty Dumpty said, in a rather scornful tone, "it means just what I choose it to mean—neither more nor less."
>
> "The question is," said Alice, "whether you can

make words mean so many different things."

"The question is," said Humpty Dumpty, "which is to be master—that's all."

People properly trained in evaluation of meta-talk can see through staged press conferences, trial balloons, press releases, programs on paper, the puppet's speech, all of which deal with problems in terms of words rather than action.

ix

WALK THROUGH LIFE, TALK WITH EVERYBODY

Talk is a process, just as life is a process. Developing and utilizing the many facets of talk will add new dimensions to your life. Talk to be effective should be flexible so that it is suitable for any situation. Many of us do not realize how intimately we are involved with the drama of talk. We are our own producer, playwright, director, and star performer. As speaker we have utilized many phrases and expressions that seem to have no obvious logical relationship to what we are saying. This is not the case. Those phrases and expressions are meaningful but in a different area and manner. As we develop a feeling and an appreciation for meta-talk, our talk should change. Its expansion will be from static to dynamic, finally becoming a process-like activity. Its structure will be made up of interactions which produce meaningful transactions. We can evolve in life from being an observer to becoming a manipulator and finally a fully involved participant. One who has passed through this growth cycle might, as an example, change his handling of criticism from "You did" to "I feel."

Many people in today's society are reluctant to talk. Some of the reasons are that the other parties seem wrong; the circumstances are improper; the time is inappropriate. There are those who fear failure. The only failure that can result from an attempt to communicate is not establishing a relationship. However you did not have one to begin with. The rewards for trying should encourage many more attempts than most of us make. With the various skills and techniques that this book has discussed it may be possible for you to take a greater risk, to get yourself into more of a life involvement. What has been discussed can by practice become more relevant and useful through the development of your insights and intuitions. The more that you use talk flavored with your judgment, the more people you will have to talk to and the more people will want to talk to you. Remember that when you talk people are no longer strangers. In fact, they are no longer "people." They become unique individuals who can help make your life immeasurably more complete.

BIBLIOGRAPHY

BAKER, RUSSELL, *Poor Russell's Almanac.* New York: Doubleday, 1972.

BARBARA, DOMINICK A., *The Art of Listening.* Springfield, Ill.: Charles C Thomas, 1965.

CHASE, STUART, *Danger: Men Talking.* New York: Parents Magazine Press, 1969.

FELDMAN, SANDOR, *Mannerisms of Speech and Gestures in Everyday Life.* New York: International Universities Press, 1959.

FLEISHMAN, ALFRED, *Sense and Nonsense—A Study in Human Communication.* San Francisco: International Society for General Semantics, 1971.

FREUD, SIGMUND, *A General Introduction to Psychoanalysis.* New York: Permabooks Ed., 1953.

GINOTT, DR. HAIM G., *Between Parent and Child.* New York: Avon, 1969.

———, *Between Parent and Teenager.* New York: Avon, 1971.

————, *Between Teacher and Child.* New York: Avon, 1973.

GOFFMAN, ERVING, *Relations in Public.* New York: Basic Books Inc., 1971.

HOVLAND, CARL I., JANIS, IRVING L., KELLEY, HAROLD H., *Communication and Persuasion.* New Haven, Conn.: Yale University Press, 1953.

JAMES, MURIEL and JONGEWARD, DOROTHY, *Born to Win.* Reading, Mass.: Addison-Wesley Publishing Co., 1971.

KORZYBSKI, ALFRED, *Science and Sanity.* Lakeville, Conn.: International Non-Aristotelian Library Publishing Co., 1958.

MACK, MARY PETER, ed., *A Bentham Reader.* New York: Pegasus, 1969.

MEHRABIAM, ALBERT, *Silent Messages.* Belmont, Calif.: Wadsworth Publishing Co., Inc., 1971.

MILLER, GEORGE A., *Language and Communication.* New York: McGraw-Hill, 1951.

NICHOLS, RALPH, AND STEVENS, LEONARD A., *Are You Listening?* New York: McGraw-Hill, 1957.

NIERENBERG, GERARD I., *Art of Negotiating.* New York: Hawthorn Books, Inc., 1968.

————, *Creative Business Negotiating.* New York: Hawthorn Books, Inc., 1971.

NIERENBERG, GERARD I., AND CALERO, HENRY, *How to Read a Person Like a Book.* New York: Hawthorn Books, Inc., 1971.

OGDEN, C. K., *Bentham's Theory of Fictions.* New Jersey: Littlefield, Adams & Co., 1959.

PARAIN, BRICE, *A Metaphysics of Language.* New York: Doubleday Anchor Books, 1971.

PEI, MARIO, *Language Today: A Survey of Current Linguistic Thought.* New York: Funk & Wagnalls, 1967.

————, *The Story of Language.* Philadelphia: J. B. Lippincott Co., 1945.

————, *Words in Sheep's Clothing.* New York: Hawthorn Books, Inc., 1969.

PERLO, F., HEFFERLINE, R., AND GOODMAN, P., *Gestalt Therapy*

—*Excitement and Growth in the Human Personality*. New York: Dell Publishing, 1951.

POSTMAN, NEIL, WEINGARTNER, CHARLES, MORAN, TERENCE P., eds., *Language in America*. New York: Pegasus, 1969.

SCHEFLEN, ALBERT, *Body Language and the Social Order*. Englewood Cliffs, N.J.: Prentice-Hall, 1972.

SHOSTROM, EVERETT, *Freedom to Be*. Englewood Cliffs, N.J.: Prentice-Hall, 1972.

SONDEL, BESS, *The Humanity of Words*. Cleveland: The World Publishing Co., 1958.

——, *To Win With Words*. New York: Hawthorn Books, 1968.

SULLIVAN, HARRY STACK, *Conceptions of Modern Psychiatry*. New York: W. W. Norton & Co., 1953.

VISCOTT, DAVID S., M.D., *How to Make Winning Your Lifestyle*. New York: Wyden, 1972.

WAGNER, GEOFFREY, *On the Wisdom of Words*. New York: Van Nostrand, 1968.

WATTS, ALAN, *Nature, Man and Woman*. New York: Pantheon, 1958.

WILLS, GARRY, *Nixon Agonistes*. New York: Signet, 1969.

INDEX OF PHRASES

About the Authors

Gerard I. Nierenberg is Founder and President of the Negotiation Institute. He is author of the books *The Art of Negotiating, Creative Business Negotiating,* and *Fundamentals of Negotiating,* and co-author with Henry Calero of *How to Read a Person Like a Book,* all with numerous foreign editions. He is a Founder of the General Semantics Foundation and President of the Institute of General Semantics Second Negotiation Institute. He is a member of the Association of the Bar of the City of New York and American Bar Association, and is a partner in the New York law firm of Nierenberg, Zeif and Weinstein. Mr. Nierenberg holds a membership in La Academía Mexicana de Derecho Internacional. He has conducted negotiations seminars worldwide.

Henry H. Calero is President of C-M Associates, a management-consulting firm which specializes in executive seminars, communications, and negotiations. He is also Executive Director of the Negotiation Institute. For many years, Mr. Calero has conducted and videotaped executive seminars for major corporations throughout the world.